BRIEF MOMENTS OF CLARITY

A Martial Arts Instructor's Guide for Living

BY

Dave Kovar

Designer: Julie Vatuone

ISBN: 13:978-1482554670

www.kovarsystems.com

DEDICATION

THIS BOOK IS DEDICATED TO YOU! You were with me as I wrote it, you know. I'm excited to share some of the ideas that have helped (and continue to help) me so much. Thank you for reading *Brief Moments of Clarity: A Martial Arts Instructor's Guide for Living.* And thank you for your reviews, Facebook comments and blog posts, too.

If my book helped you and you would like to help others by sharing it, please consider reviewing *Brief Moments of Clarity* on your faviorite book sales sites. Reviews are the best way to share the good news! They're fast and easy to do. Just go to the book on the site, and add your review. Thank you so much.

And ... congratulations! You wouldn't be holding this book right now if you hadn't decided to take action to move forward in your life. To your health, happiness and success!

FORWARD BY MOM AND DAD

FROM MY MOM, Lorraine Kovar—Retired School Teacher, Administrator and Proud Mother

Brief Moments of Clarity: A Martial Artist's Guide for Living is an insightful book—it beautifully adapts the concepts of martial arts to improving relationship and leadership skills in almost all areas of life.

Dave speaks and writes from a long career of teaching and relating positively to people of all ages. He is artful in describing difficult or unfortunate situations with others and then giving simple, yet profound, ways of solving the problem in a sensitive and positive way. I recommend this book to those interested in improving their personal and professional relationships.

FROM MY DAD, Len Kovar—Retired Minister, Counselor, Author, WWII Veteran and Proud Father

Is there a reason, a point to life and the human adventure, beyond that of simply living and, perhaps, becoming rich and famous?

Philosophers and thinkers of every age suggest that there is a higher objective than merely fame and fortune for all of us. This loftier goal has to do with becoming more of a whole and integrated person—a human being who has more fully actualized his potential to grow toward the wholeness that he or she might become and embrace. To attain such a lofty goal is a major accomplishment. And only a very few individuals ever get there.

In this book, my son shares his spirit and the footsteps he has taken along the way—as well as the principles he has learned, developed and demonstrated as a Martial Artist—to grow toward greater fulfillment as a human being.

Brief Moments of Clarity: A Martial Arts Instructor's Guide for Living brings forth attitudes, techniques and activities that lead to greater wholeness as an evolving person. This kind of fulfillment is the truest measure of a successful life.

I warmly and fully recommend this book. It will add depth and wholeness to all who seek to become a more complete, positive and well-rounded human being.

"Try to learn to breathe deeply, really to taste food when you eat, and when you sleep really to sleep. Try as much as possible to be wholly alive with all your might, and when you laugh, laugh like hell."

— **William Saroyan, Author**

67 | CHAPTER 3

WHEN THINGS ARE TOUGH

86 | CHAPTER 4

MAKING A DIFFERENCE

INTRODUCTION

HI! I AM A PROFESSIONAL Martial Arts instructor. I love to teach! And I love what Martial Arts does for people of all ages and abilities ... how it makes them strive to grow ... how it gives them more confidence than they had before ... and how that confidence pours into every aspect of their lives.

I also like the fact that Martial Arts teaches people practical self-defense skills. It's nice to know that you can defend yourself against the bad guy, if and when you were to encounter him. And because of the added confidence that Martial Arts training brings, most trained people are less likely to be confronted because of the confidence they project. We say, "Practice the fight so you don't have to." The reality is, however, that most people will never need to defend themselves against a bad guy in a dark alley. Sure, it might happen, but chances are pretty rare.

But there is another kind of self-defense that we all need to learn and practice in order to lead healthy, happy and productive lives—the defense against everyday occurrences such as sickness, injury, others' and our own bad attitudes, poor self-discipline and apathy (just to name a few).

Every now and then, I have a brief moment of clarity ... a moment when everything comes into focus. When this happens, I feel as if I can accomplish anything I want to accomplish. But there is a proving ground, a time to put these moments into practice, in order to reap their rewards and be ready for the next opportunity to learn.

If there are diamonds in this book, they began as lumps of coal. It was only with the intense pressure and heat of challenging circumstances did they become valuable to me.

Brief Moments of Clarity comprises some of the most valuable lessons I've learned so far during my life's journey. Some of these brief moments of clarity were born of many years of trial and refinement. I've worked to apply them to being the best husband, dad, son, brother, friend, teacher and business owner that I can be. And, yes, I've made a lot of mistakes—I still do—but that's how we learn, right? The key is to L-E-A-R-N. It's an honor to share some of my *Brief Moments of Clarity* with you!

CHAPTER 1—The Mastery Mindsets

EVERYONE FACES CHALLENGES. Some challenges are bigger than others but, regardless of size, every challenge that we face has the potential either to help us get to the next level or stop us in our tracks ... depending on how we respond to it. *The Mastery Mindsets* are made up of nine power affirmations designed to help retrain the way we think about and respond to the challenges that come our way.

The Mastery Mindsets connect the dots so that we can live our lives more proactively and powerfully. The key to internalizing *The Mastery Mindsets* is to focus on one mindset at a time until it becomes part of you. If you do this, there'll come a time when one of *The Mastery Mindsets* pops into your head just when you need it. The moment that happens, your life will have just changed forever. You will realize that you are in charge. That's powerful. But as you're learning, don't try to do too much too soon. Just take it one *Mastery Mindset* at a time. (If you'd like some more ideas on how to really make *The Mastery Mindsets* your own, check out the BONUS section at the end of this book—Putting *The Mastery Mindset*s to Work With the *Daily 3x3s*.) With some time and patience, great things will happen.

The Mastery Mindsets

I can. I will.

This challenge will make me stronger.

I deflect negative energy.

I accept positive energy.

I remain calm, even in challenging situations.

My word is law.

I'm running my own race.

I bring value to all of my relationships.

I have so much to be thankful for.

LET'S GET STARTED!

Mastery Mindset—WEEK 1

I can. I will.

. . . .

DESCRIPTION

This *Mastery Mindset* refers to your Attitude, Belief and Commitment. It is an affirmation that you WILL get through any challenge that you are currently facing. It is about being stubborn in a positive way. Allow me to illustrate this mindset with the following story.

. . . .

ILLUSTRATION

Many years ago, I was wandering through Sears when I stumbled upon a treadmill that happened to be the exact one my wife wanted. It was on sale, so I bought it on the spot. But when I brought my receipt to the warehouse for pick-up, the clerk asked me what kind of vehicle I was driving. It hadn't occurred to me until that moment that I had driven my brand new, bright red Mazda Miata to Sears that day. When I told the clerk, he said there was no way that I would be able to get my treadmill home in that car.

Normally, I would have agreed. But there was something in his voice caused me to take fitting the treadmill into my small car on as a challenge. I knew that, somehow, I would get the treadmill home … no doubt about it.

With the top down and the treadmill hanging several inches over the side of the car and a few feet out the back, I drove out of the Sears parking lot. I couldn't see at all to the right of me and I could only use first and third gears, since the box was jammed up against my stick shift. But I made it home. When I stopped at red lights, I saw the other drivers shake their heads in disbelief.

Now, I'm not claiming that it was a very bright thing to do. And I would probably try to discourage friends from attempting a similar endeavor today. But I think my triumph perfectly illustrates the concept of I CAN. I WILL. At some time in our lives, each one of us has shown our ability to be stubborn, refuse to take no for an answer, and be fully committed to the completion of a task.

As for me, being stubborn comes naturally. It's the way I'm wired. Now to put my stubbornness and determination to work in the right ways for the right reasons. Instead of insisting on carting home an eight-foot long treadmill in a pocket-size car, can I insist on teaching the very best class possible? Can I refuse to lower my standards regarding my diet and exercise habits? Can I be absolutely committed to taking care of my team, my family and my community? I don't always get it right, but I'm working on it.

· ·

CHALLENGE

What about you? What are you stubborn about? What are you fully committed to? I challenge you to take some time to figure this out. In some ways, you're probably just as stubborn as I am. Are you channeling this attribute in the right direction or wasting it on trivialities and maybe letting it impact others or you negatively? I challenge you to adopt the first *Mastery Mindset*—I CAN. I WILL. And then apply it to the things that matter most to you.

MASTERY MINDSET—WEEK 2

This challenge will make me stronger.

. . . .

DESCRIPTION

Chances are you've heard these or similar quotes before:
Good timber doesn't grow with ease, the stronger the wind, the stronger the trees (J. Willard Marriott). *Calm seas make for sorry sailors* (Mexican Proverb). Perhaps you've even shared one with someone you know who was going through hard times. It's always easy to give advice to other people who are struggling. Although I may phrase it gently, I'm really saying, "Suck it up. Quit whining. You'll get through this and you'll be better for it." However, it's a little tougher to apply this concept—THIS CHALLENGE WILL MAKE ME STRONGER—to my own life. After all, when I'm the one going through the tough times, it's different. Right? Not really. I needed a shift to occur in my own thinking, so I created this *Mastery Mindset*— THIS CHALLENGE WILL MAKE ME STRONGER. And it worked!

When you look at some of your past challenges, you can probably see how you benefited from them and how they helped to shape you into the person you are now. As a matter fact, you are probably even thankful for some of your most difficult challenges because of all the blessings they brought. Sure, they might not have seemed wonderful at the time but, in retrospect, you can see all the good that came from them. I can think of so many instances in my life where this is true, but I'd like to share one experience, in particular, with you.

. . . .

ILLUSTRATION

I grew up in a Martial Arts school. My first job was teaching karate. I opened up my own school six months out of high school. And life was good. After a few years, I decided to get serious about my business. I borrowed money from family and moved to a bigger, more expensive location. This is when things became challenging for me very quickly. The extra pressure was taking its toll on me and I started to doubt my choice of vocations.

One day during a particularly challenging month, a gentleman came in off the street and offered to buy my school from me. Without thinking twice about it, I sold the school. But instead of taking the money and paying all my debts, I bought a Porsche. The Porsche broke down shortly after I bought it and I sold it for next to nothing. All of a sudden, I found myself without my Martial Arts school and with all the debt that I incurred along the way. Out of desperation, I took a job painting low-income housing units.

It didn't take me too long to realize how many poor choices I had made. And it took me nearly four years until I was in a financial position to reopen my school on a full-time basis. During those years painting apartments, a day did not go by when I didn't want to kick myself for being so stupid. How could I have sold my school without thinking it through? Why didn't I pay off my debts instead of buying that car?

Looking back, however, I could not be more thankful for the experience. I wouldn't trade it for anything … now! I learned the value of keeping my debt low and the importance of having good credit. I now deeply appreciate and respect how hard it is to have a 'real job.' But most importantly, this experience helped me to realize how lucky I am to make my living doing something I love.

While there are plenty of challenges that go along with my profession, I only have to remember walking up three flights of stairs while carrying two 5-gallon buckets of paint into a cockroach infested apartment in 100-degree weather to do sheetrock repair, whenever I start to second-guess what I do. This helps me to let go of feeling sorry for myself and rapidly return to feeling extremely grateful for my profession.

CHALLENGE

"This challenge will make me stronger" is an excellent affirmation to use when you have to navigate rough waters. It reminds us of the importance of *optimism* and *resiliency*—and it can help us keep a healthy perspective and stay focused on solutions. I challenge you to put this strategy to work in your life.

MASTER MINDSET—WEEK 3

I deflect negative energy.

. . . .

DESCRIPTION

"I deflect negative energy" refers to the importance of not letting situations or people steal your joy. Have you ever been having a great day until somebody said something negative that threw you off your game?

. . . .

ILLUSTRATION

When I reflect on this mindset now, it reminds me of an experience I had teaching a self-defense clinic to a group of women. Everything went really well during the class. Afterwards, I received a lot of great feedback ... mostly. One woman pulled me aside and let me have it with both barrels. She directed at me what seemed like a lifetime of anger because she felt that, as a male, I was unqualified to teach women's self-defense.

For several hours afterwards, I let her steal my joy. Rather than focus on the great feedback I received from the majority of the participants, I concentrated on the comments from that one woman.

It's easy to say, "You shouldn't let her bother you!" when you're giving advice to your friends. The challenge is to follow that advice in your own life. Here are a few strategies that work well for me. Perhaps they'll do the same for you.

First, do your best to avoid negative environments. This may seem like common sense, but we can let our guard down without realizing it. And reminders never hurt.

A gentleman once came into my school to ask about taking a self-defense class. What a sight! He had a black eye, fat lip and some stitches on his cheek. Come to find out, he had just been in a bar fight and lost. (I'm not sure if there is a winning side in a bar fight, but we'll talk about that another time). He told me that he wanted to learn some self-defense because every time he went to this one particular bar, he always got into a fight. I responded half-jokingly by saying, "Well then, don't go to that bar!"

"I hadn't thought of that. What a great idea!" he said.

Are there any metaphorical "bars" in your life that you should not go into anymore?

Another preventative aspect of **"I DEFLECT NEGATIVE ENERGY"** is to do your best to steer clear of negative people. We've all experienced our share of these, I'm sure. But one gentleman, in particular, clearly stands out. The father of one of our young students, he spent a couple hours each week waiting in our lobby while his son was in class.

BRIEF MOMENTS OF CLARITY

Once when I shook his hand and asked him how he was doing, he replied, "Lousy, but thanks for asking." I was a little surprised, but figured he was just having a bad day. Over time, however, I found that every day was a bad day for him. Virtually every conversation I had with him was negative. Life was hard. He was sick. His son was dumb. We needed to teach better classes, etc.

For a while, I tried to pierce through his negativity and cheer him up, but it was never enough. Eventually, I realized that this is who he chooses to be. After that, I waved to him as I passed and gave him a smile, but never slowed down long enough to have a conversation so I wouldn't have to subject myself to a bunch of negativity. Of course, it's impossible to avoid negative people all the time, but I bet that you can avoid them a lot more than you do.

Perhaps the most important strategy is not to take things personally. As a Martial Arts instructor, I know that it's rarely the students' fault when I lose patience. It usually has to do with the fact that I'm thinking about something else at the time—something that irritates me—and the students just happen to be in front of me (so I unconsciously take out my frustrations on them).

With this in mind, I understand now that the woman who lit into me at the self-defense clinic had some challenges that she was trying to work through—and that she was trying to resolve her issues by venting at me. Her anger probably didn't have anything to do with me at all! It wasn't personal. I hope that I won't let it get to me, if I find myself in a similar situation.

. . . .

CHALLENGE

So the next time some negative energy gets thrown your way, simply do your best to deflect it. Remember the childhood jingle, "I'm rubber, you're glue | Whatever you say bounces off of me and sticks to you." Yeah! I didn't realize it at the time, but now I'd say that's pretty good advice for dealing with negativity.

MASTER MINDSET—WEEK 4

I accept positive energy.

. . . .

DESCRIPTION

People can be their own hardest critics. We give ourselves unwarranted negative feedback way too often, in addition to healthy constructive criticism. And we often graciously accept others' constructive criticism, even if we disagree with it. If we're learners, we can be grateful for merited feedback and do our best to absorb it, learn from it, and do better next time. However, many of us don't do as well accepting positive feedback.

I'm guessing that I'm not the only one who has sloughed off a compliment from a friend, instead of soaking in their kind words and sincerely thanking them. *The Mastery Mindset* "I ACCEPT POSITIVE ENERGY" is about being receptive to kindness and appreciation. To accept positive energy is to make a conscious choice to accept and celebrate positive feedback from others as a gift, rather than downplay it. C'mon, we hear enough negativity everyday. When we hear some good stuff, let's absorb it. Let's enjoy it! Remember, a person is giving you a gift when he or she pays you a compliment. Don't you think that a sincere "Thank You" is in order, rather than refusing to take the gift or dropping it and walking away?

Another way to surround ourselves with uplifting energy is to integrate with optimistic people and an upbeat environment. Theoretically, we all know this but are we doing it? I once heard Tony Robbins say, "Stand guard at the door of your mind." His advice was to be careful about what you let into your head because it can't help but affect you in some way. So it follows that to keep a watchful eye over our thoughts, we need to stand guard and be very selective of the people with whom we keep company, as well as the environments in which we spend our time.

. . . .

ILLUSTRATION

Turning fifty is often considered to be an important birthday because it signifies the halfway point to one hundred years old. I, personally, have never taken birthdays too seriously, though. So when my fiftieth came around, it was just business as usual … that is, until I started getting a ton of congratulatory comments from friends, coworkers and family members.

While I always thanked people for their congratulations, I never internalized them. Instead, I just let them roll off of me and fall by the wayside. But one evening, my wife Angelina and I were on the way to dinner when a friend called to wish me, "Happy Birthday!" I responded sarcastically with a random comment like, "Yeah, whatever," glibly thanked him, and then hung up.

Angelina looked at me. "From what I just overheard, it seems to me that you didn't really accept his well wishes," she said. "Your birthday is still a few days away. Why don't you make it a point to really accept all the great energy people are sending your way, instead of just blowing them off? You only turn fifty once, you know." Her comment was perfect and made complete sense. From that moment forward, I decided that every time someone wished me a "Happy Birthday," I would take a moment to really hear it, and appreciate and accept the positive energy they were sending my way. This had an amazingly positive effect on me, one I will remember. Since then, I have been making a more conscious effort to try to accept positive thoughts when they're sent my way. Care to join me?

· ·

CHALLENGE

Make a deliberate choice to spend time with optimistic people. Read inspiring books. Go to uplifting places. Find ways to be of service to others and bring value to the lives of those around you. When you surround yourself with positives, you'll be reenergized. And when you let yourself feel that renewed energy, you'll fully understand the power of "I ACCEPT POSITIVE ENERGY." I challenge you to fully integrate "I ACCEPT POSITIVE ENERGY" into your life. There is no downside and a lot to gain.

MASTER MINDSET—WEEK 5

I remain calm, even in challenging situations.

. . . .

DESCRIPTION

Who is a mighty person? There are lots of ways to answer this question, but my favorite response is that a mighty person is one who has control of their emotions.

My father is sage, with over fifty years experience as a counselor and minister. I once told him how I wished I could control my emotions all the time, but that it was difficult. I also shared with him that I get angry with myself for being angry. It was then that he said something very profound to me.

My dad told me the first step to controlling my emotions is to acknowledge and accept the emotion I'm experiencing and, if I can do that, I'd be halfway there. The second step is to decide on a course of action (which usually means, when you're angry, to try to be calm and not say or do anything stupid).

His advice marked a subtle turning point for me. Afterwards, I would say to myself, "I remain calm, even in challenging situations." This affirmation has become very powerful for me. In my experience, the easiest way to increase self-control is to practice "I REMAIN CALM, EVEN IN CHALLENGING SITUATIONS" when you are faced with everyday issues.

For example, the next time you open up the refrigerator and the orange juice falls off the top shelf and spills all over the floor, simply take a deep breath and say, "I remain calm, even in challenging situations." Then quietly clean up the mess. As you practice, remaining calm will become easier … even with major issues.

I still get irritated or angry sometimes. But now I am usually aware that my color is rising—and this awareness minimizes the effect those negative emotions have on me.

. . . .

ILLUSTRATION

I attended a Waldorf high school. The school's guiding philosophy towards education is based on the teachings of Rudolf Steiner, a brilliant thinker who had a different, more holistic view of education than his contemporaries. The Waldorf methodology emphasizes immersing students in one subject for several weeks at a time. This is called the Main Lesson. At the end of each *Main Lesson*, the students are required to turn in their Main Lesson Book—an in-depth, term paper with illustrations.

I had a particularly challenging main lesson at one point during my senior year. I had been working really hard on my main lesson book for weeks and was quite proud of it. Two days before the due date, the unthinkable happened—my

Main Lesson Book vanished! I never found out what happened to it. I searched everywhere, but no book. All that I found were some rough notes and a few of my drawings. I was frantic. What was I going to do?

Upset, I told my mother that I wasn't going to turn in anything and would take an incomplete, cross my fingers, and hope that I could still graduate with my class. Calm and composed, my mom quietly listened. When the time was right, she said, "Dave, take a deep breath. Let's just think this through. Do you really think that not turning in anything is a good idea? Perhaps we should try to recreate your book from scratch. I'll bet you that if you can calm down and focus, you will get it done in time."

Seventeen year olds don't often listen to their mothers, but this time I did. I started over. Several times along the way, I'd get frustrated. My mom would then remind me to be calm and breathe. I finally finished my Main Lesson Book. It was pretty good. In fact, it was probably better than my original.

To this day, when I find myself in a challenging situation and start to lose it or feel frustrated, I think of Mom telling me to "breathe and be calm." This simple approach has transformed my life. Thanks, Mom, for this valuable lesson (one of many).

CHALLENGE

The next time you find yourself in a challenging situation and you feel like you are about to come unglued, take a deep breath and then make a concentrated effort to remain calm. Practice with the little things and then work you way up.

MASTER MINDSET—WEEK 6

My word is law.

. . . .

DESCRIPTION

"My word is law" is a great concept to strengthen self-discipline. Simply put, "MY WORD IS LAW" is about keeping the commitments you've made to yourself. Easier said than done, right? Most people fail to develop a high level of self-discipline because they commit to too much, too soon. It becomes way too hard to keep so many commitments, so they give up and go back to their old ways.

. . . .

ILLUSTRATION

Although I have exercised early in the morning for most of my adult life, it's still not easy to get up and get going. I want to blow off my workout and sleep a little longer sometimes. Some evenings before I go to bed, if I sense that I'm going to have a hard time getting up in the morning, I look myself in the mirror and tell myself out loud, "You are getting up and going to the gym in the morning. My word is law. Just do it. Even if you don't feel like it." Inevitably, when morning arrives and I don't want to wake up, I remember what I told myself the night before. That's usually all it takes. After my workout, I take a few moments to celebrate and anchor in the good feeling of the workout and how glad I am that I did it. This makes getting up the next morning a little bit easier.

. . . .

CHALLENGE

Choose something positive that you'd like to become a habit. Keep it simple. For example, flossing your teeth or replacing a candy bar with an apple as your late-night treat. Then look in the mirror and tell yourself out loud, "For the next week I'm going to ... My word is law." Experiencing success is important to building self-discipline, so begin with small commitments and build on them.

MASTER MINDSET—WEEK 7

I'm running my own race.

. . . .

DESCRIPTION

I'm not sure how it is in other countries, but I know that people in America are competitive. We can't help it. We were raised that way—good ol' American ingenuity, hard work, and a competitive spirit. Like it or not, we've been competing since birth. How much did your child weigh when she was born? How old was your son when he began to walk? When did you start writing a bike? How early did you learn to read? You get the idea.

I'm not against competition. Within the right context, competition has its place and can be very valuable. But an unhealthy approach to competition instills in us the destructive habit of always comparing ourselves with others. I see it in the Martial Arts profession all the time. School owners compare statistics with other school owners—how many students they have, how many black belts they have promoted, how much their business grosses every month, etc.

But comparing yourself with others just doesn't work. In Hamlet, Shakespeare wrote, "Comparisons are odious [contemptible]." Modeling success and trying to learn from those around you are much different than comparing yourself to others. Remember, we are all running our own races. When you compare yourself with others, you will perceive yourself as either better or worse in some respect. And what good comes from that? Would you compare an apple to a pencil and ask which one is better? Of course not. It wouldn't make sense. If you needed to write, the pencil would be better, but if you were hungry, an apple would be your preference. And what if you were hungry and needed to write? Both would be valuable to you.

This sounds reasonable, but against whom or what are you going to measure yourself? With whom do you compete? Run your own race. Compare yourself to y*our own potential.* How do we know what our own potential is? *Your potential* is what you think you can do when you are at your very best. *Your potential* is the goals you set for yourself when you were feeling inspired and motivated.

Have you ever felt dejected because you felt someone was better than you were at *something*? Someone else may have an impressive achievement and that's great, but it doesn't have anything to do with you. It's okay to be aware of the achievements and aptitudes of others, but don't dwell on them. Instead, focus on what you can do to be your very best. There are so many different ways to be successful in life. Each one of us is different. Each of us needs to set our own goals and strive to be the very best we can be. We have to find our own way, figure out what's right for us, and then strive to do the best we can with the resources we have. Whether or not we realize it, we're all running our own race.

ILLUSTRATION

I had a friend with whom I was always comparing myself. It didn't matter what the activity was—athletics, academics, or even music—he was always better than me at everything. I spent an entire school year just trying to beat him at something, anything, but never did. A lot of the time, he didn't even know that I was competing with him. It was extremely frustrating because, no matter what I did, I never seemed to measure up. He always won.

But one day, he told me in confidence how unhappy he was with himself … that life was hard for him … that he felt unbearable pressure to win all the time … and that he was suicidal. I had no idea. I had assumed that he lived in a perpetual state of bliss and that everything came naturally and easily to him.

This new snapshot of my 'perfect' friend really changed my perspective about everything. It helped me to realize that we're all struggling and striving, regardless of external appearances or our perspective on someone. After that day, I quit comparing myself to my friend for good. My envy was replaced with compassion.

Eventually, with the help of his family, some counseling and a lot of soul-searching on his part, he made it through. Today, he is confident and happy with a rewarding career and a loving family. Although we don't see each other very often, we are still good friends.

Have I stopped comparing myself to others altogether? No. There are still plenty of times when I fall into that trap. But I catch myself quickly now and refuse to go there. After all, "I AM RUNNING MY OWN RACE."

. . . .

CHALLENGE

The next time you find yourself comparing yourself with someone else, stop and take a moment to remind yourself that comparing yourself with other people is a complete waste of time. Remember that you are "running your own race." Instead, use the time you would have spent worrying about what someone else can do to improve yourself.

MASTERY MINDSET—WEEK 8

I bring value to all my relationships.

. . . .

DESCRIPTION

"I bring value to all my relationships" is a continual reminder of the importance of empathy, respect, patience and service. Very few people would disagree with this ... in theory. But in practice, well that's a different story. I want to share a simple experience that illustrates the importance of bringing value to all our relationships.

. . . .

ILLUSTRATION

I found myself waiting in an extremely long line at the checkout counter one Saturday, just before Christmas. (Apparently, I wasn't the only one who was doing some last minute Christmas shopping.) And there was only one person working the cash register. There were eight people ahead of me and nobody was happy with the situation. The tension was so thick that you could almost see a gray aura of negativity gushing out of the line towards the undeserving cashier.

Unfortunately, I joined the fray and had become part of the mob mentality that was brewing. I felt impatient and indignant and tried to catch the cashier's eye to communicate this. Eventually, she did glance up from the register long enough for our eyes to meet. It wasn't long (only a fraction of a second), but it was long enough for me to completely change my perspective. With just that quick look, I saw her as a conscientious but overwhelmed person who was doing her best under stressful circumstances. She was trying to get through the day, working as hard as she could in a thankless job. This brief connection made me even more aware of the negativity being sent her way by the impatient crowd. But this time, I did not contribute negativity to the drama. In fact, I found myself wanting to help her, bring her some much needed compassion, and make her smile.

Amazingly, the line began to move faster when my attitude changed. When I reached the cash register, she looked up and forced a smile, undoubtedly expecting me to glare at her. Instead, I smiled at her and hoped that I could find the right words. I jokingly told her that she was personally responsible for not only the long line in the store but for the traffic outside, as well. She flashed me a relieved smile. You could almost feel her tension dissolving. I then thanked her for being so patient with all of us grumpy customers, and told her how I thought she was doing a great job and that the store was lucky to have her. As I was leaving the store our eyes crossed and she mouthed, "Thank you," and then happily turned back to the next person in line. I knew she felt better and so did I.

It's amazing what a little bit of kindness can do for everyone involved. I can do better still. Sometimes I slip up, but I'm working on it. What I've found, though, is that kindness is an addiction. Once you taste a little, you want more. Kindness is one addiction that is good for everyone. So won't you join me in some random acts of kindness? But beware, kindness is highly contagious!

. . . .

CHALLENGE

Consider going out of your way to do something nice for a few select people in your life—maybe for a family member, a coworker or a complete stranger. Remember to go outside your comfort zone and do something different, something unexpected. Don't expect anything in return. Don't do it for recognition or gratitude. Do it because it is the right thing to do. In doing this, you'll be reminded that bringing joy to others is the easiest way to bring more joy into your own life.

MASTERY MINDSET—WEEK 9

I have so much to be thankful for!

. . . .

DESCRIPTION

While we all want to improve our lives and meet our challenges, we need to be careful not to lose perspective of all the great things going on in our lives.

. . . .

ILLUSTRATION

I have so much for which to be grateful—a wonderful wife, two great kids, excellent health and a rewarding career. As a matter of fact, probably ninety-seven percent of my life is absolutely perfect. In my better moments, I know this. The challenge is that I'm not always in one of my better moments. When I'm not, I find myself focusing on the three percent that isn't so great. Why would I give these miserable three percent ninety seven percent of my attention?

Sometimes, I can let a trivial thing get in the way of a great day. For example, I jumped in the shower one morning to discover that we had no hot water. It was late November and I was cold even before those little icy droplets took the breath out of me. And then I was drenched in freezing cold water. It took a blow dryer, a wool blanket and a whole lot of hot tea before I could get my lips back to their normal color.

I whined about it all morning. It took a couple of days before we could coordinate the repair work on our water heater. Boy, did I miss my hot shower!

The good news was that I found myself profoundly appreciative of this little modern miracle we call *hot running water*. This gratitude lasted about a week, when I slipped back to taking having hot water on demand for granted.

But sometimes I remember. I take a moment to reflect on how wonderful it is to twist a knob and have clean, hot water stream down my back. Then I get to pondering what else I have in my life, here and now, that I might be taking for granted. I can tell you that my list of what I have is extremely long. And I bet your list is just as long.

Well, I'm off to breakfast. I am so lucky! I have a device in my kitchen that keeps all my food cold until I'm ready to use it! Pretty cool, huh? Yet another thing to add to my list …

CHALLENGE

I challenge you, as I'm challenging myself, to take some time every day to think about all the things in your life for which you're grateful. There are a lot, for sure, but you have to be pay attention to see them. Here's a great way to put this to work:

1. Make a list of everything you have to be thankful for. Big things, little things. People, experiences, conveniences … everything. Give it this title: "I Have a Good Life Filled With All of These Things I'm Thankful For."

2. Once you've written your list, take a good long look at it.

3. Put it in an envelope and seal it.

4. Give it to a friend and ask them to hang onto it and give it back to you at some point in the future when you're going through a very hard time.

Seeing your list in your handwriting when you're highly focused on your problems will remind you that, in spite of your challenges, you really do have so much to be thankful for.

CHAPTER 2: SATORI, IN THE MOMENT … AT YOUR BEST

SATORI IS A JAPANESE WORD that roughly translates into *"A Moment of Deep Understanding."* For use in our business, we took the original meaning and modified it to mean *"In the moment … At your best."*

Satori is that state of mental clarity, physical energy and emotional calm. Satori is the ideal performance state. Satori is being in the zone.

Imagine what would happen if you spent the majority of your life in this state. Wow! Is maintaining Satori easy? Of course not. Is it a worthy goal? Absolutely. Living mindfully will help us to maximize the amount of time we spend at our best.

The following stories are some of my Satori moments where I discovered, practiced and learned a little more about being *in the moment … at my best.*

Flying keeps you humble.

I'M PRETTY SURE THAT I TRAVEL enough to qualify me for frequent flyer status. While flying can be quite stressful (if you're not careful), you can learn a lot of life lessons in airports. And emotional composure is definitely one of them!

When I'm flying, I pride myself in not overreacting to things out of my control— such as late flights, broken planes, lost luggage and middle seats. I often find myself watching in amazement as someone chews out a gate agent because the flight is canceled or yells at the flight attendant because the plane is delayed. When I observe one of these emotional outbursts, I usually pat myself on the back because I'm so above such behavior … or so I thought.

Here's what happened. I was waiting in line to board a plane when the woman ahead of me was asked to condense her three pieces of luggage down to two, as is the law. The woman stormed off, completely indignant, mumbling something inappropriate under her breath. I thought to myself, "There is another outburst. Doesn't she know that the gate agent is just doing her job? She looks so silly losing her temper. I would never behave like that."

When it was my turn to show my ticket, the gate agent looked down at my bag and said, "That looks a little big. Do you mind checking to see if it will fit in the container over there before you board?"

Before I knew it, I found myself storming off in the general direction of the plane and mumbling, "I travel all the time. I know what I'm doing. Can't she seew that? Of course it will fit. The nerve of some people!"

Then it hit me. "Wow, I just did the same thing that I was passing judgment on a few seconds ago. It looks like I have a bit more work to do than I thought. I guess I have a way to go on the emotional composure front after all."

This minor incident was a major reminder not to pass judgment on others, but to use that same energy to improve myself instead. By the way, my bag didn't fit in the container. "That darn gate agent. Doesn't she know … ?" Oops, there I go again. Happy travels!

If being upset and angry helps, then go for it!

WHEN I WAS IN MY MID-TWENTIES, I lost my wallet at the beach. I was very upset at the hassle this created—applying for a new driver's license, canceling my credit cards, and trying to recreate my address book … plus all the other annoying little things that go along with losing a wallet.

I expressed my frustration to my Dad, expecting him to console me. But instead, he said, "If being upset and angry about losing your wallet helps you get through it any better or faster, then be really angry or upset. But if it doesn't help, why not try to take the emotion out of it and just do what you have to do?" At the time, I didn't like his advice. But it has served me well since then.

So, the next time you find yourself angry with or upset by a situation, ask yourself this simple question, "Will this emotion help me get through this situation any easier and without any long term ramifications?" If the answer is "yes"—and it rarely is—then, by all means, be really upset and angry. But if the answer is "no," try your best to regain your emotional composure and then do what you have to do to resolve the issue in a calm and rational way.

Just wipe it off.

YEARS AGO, MY WIFE ANGELINA DECIDED that it was time to go back to work. The kids were older and needed her less. After fifteen years of homemaking, she wanted to know whether or not she still had what it took to be out there in the 'real world.'

So she decided to get back to her passion … teaching preschoolers. It is a rare person who can wipe noses, kiss boo-boos, and play with blocks for several hours a day … and enjoy it. Not only does Angela survive in this environment, she thrives. She comes home every day with cute stories of how much fun she had with "her" kids, how they made her laugh and, sometimes, how they made her cry.

She had one student, a little girl named Maria, who was a real handful. She invited confrontation—playmate, teacher, parent, it didn't matter. Maria loved a good argument. She enjoyed dishing it out. She once told Angela with great enthusiasm, "I love being bad." Maria could take confrontation pretty well, too. No other child seemed to be able to ruffle her feathers.

One time, Angelina came home with a great Maria story. Apparently, several kids were ganging up on Maria and calling her names because she wouldn't share the red tricycle. They called her every mean name that a group of three year olds could think of—"booger-head," "sissy" and "potty pants," to name a few. Normally, such name-calling would elicit tears or sand throwing or *something* … but not with Maria. She simply looked up and said with complete composure, "I don't care what you say to me because I JUST WIPE IT OFF." And then she pretended to wipe something off of her shoulder and rode away as carefree as ever on the red tricycle.

As Maria grows up, I hope she learns to share more. I hope she can learn to at least *like* being good, if not love it. I hope that she can find joy in friendship. But I also hope that she never loses her ability to *wipe it off* and ride away carefree on her red tricycle when people or circumstances are trying to bring her down.

Next time you find yourself being called a "booger-head" or the equivalent, ask yourself, "What would Maria do?" I will, too.

Don't speak out of anger.

I'VE MADE THE FOLLOWING TWO STATEMENTS my personal mantras:

> *Don't speak out of anger.*
> *Logic and emotion are like oil and water; they don't mix.*

Heck, I've preached these to anyone that would listen for as long as I can remember. While I've made some progress, I still have a ways to go.

For example, I happen to catch one of our children's classes improperly staffed one day and didn't bother to ask why. Instead, I gave the instructor a piece of my mind. And, of course, the self-justification for being angry set in.

"But this is different," I think. "It should be addressed immediately. The safety of the kids is at stake," I told myself, but not really believing it. "I'm calm. Honestly, I just need to get this off of my chest before I explode."

So there I flew, tying into a couple of hard-working, conscientious instructors who happened to be doing their best. They apologized. It shouldn't have happened. They will make sure it doesn't happen in the future. Et cetera. I felt a sense of power as I strutted off. I sure showed them who's boss!

As is so often the case, I quickly found out the real story. One of the scheduled instructors had had a legitimate emergency and couldn't come to work. To solve this problem, the instructor solicited the help of another staff member who wasn't scheduled to teach that class. There is a portion of each class during which the instructor divides the students into smaller groups to practice specific things. What I had seen was the only chunk of class that wasn't fully staffed. They had done the best they could with the resources they had. I had some apologizing to do.

Next time, I will behave differently. I will hold my temper. (At least, I hope I will.) Whenever I become emotional and speak out of anger, I end up regretting it. Next time, I will try to remember:

Don't speak out of anger.
Logic and emotion are like oil and water; they don't mix.

. . . .

Just because someone told you so, it doesn't make it true.

EARLY IN MY CAREER as a Martial Arts instructor, I found it necessary to supplement my income by taking a day job painting apartments. My boss' name was Paul. My initial feeling about him was very positive and I felt like he was going to be a good boss.

On my first day on the job, Paul partnered me with Toby, who was to be my trainer and show me the ropes. Toby seemed like a pretty good guy and I liked him right away. Within a few hours, we became fast friends. But when he felt he had my trust, he started complaining about what a lousy boss Paul was. He told me I should check my timecard and paycheck ... that it wasn't above Paul to try to cheat his employees if he could get away with it. While I was uncomfortable with Toby sharing this with me, I had no reason to doubt him. So I began to look for signs that Paul had cheated me. I saw none.

Within a few days of working alongside Toby, I began to notice things about him that made me uncomfortable. He padded his timecard and wanted me to do the same. I refused. He also included things we never did on our worksheet. It soon became apparent that Toby was the liar, not Paul. Paul fired Toby in my first month with the company.

I continued to work for Paul for several years. Always in the corner of my mind, I watched for that dishonest guy Toby had warned me about to show up. But he never did. Paul was a great boss—hardworking, ethical and as honest as the day is long. We are good friends to this day.

Toby's initial comments took years to undo! Whenever I hear someone say something negative about someone else, I remember that, "Just because someone told you so, it doesn't make it true."

Thanks, Toby, for the great lesson. More importantly, thank you, Paul, for being a great example!

It's just a matter of perspective.

EVERY NOW AND THEN, the universe finds a strange way to put everything into perspective and provide us with a glimpse of just how good we really have it. I would like to share a story that did just that for me.

A few years back I bought *a really nice little sports car* at the auto auction for fifty cents on the dollar. It was beautiful … gold on gold, ragtop, fully loaded. I loved that car. There was just one problem with it. The back seat really was more like a large glove compartment with seatbelts than it was a place for passengers to ride in. With two kids and plenty of carpooling duties, it just didn't cut it. I had to get something larger, so I settled on four-door sedan. For a while, I kept the sports car, too. It was such a fun car to drive and I was having a hard time parting with it.

One day while backing out of the garage, I managed to scratch the entire left side of my sports car with the right side of my new sedan. In an instant, both cars became body shop bound. Upon realizing what I had done, my immediate response was to get extremely angry. How could this have happened! This is going to cost a fortune! I can't believe that … Then it hit me. My biggest problem in life is that I backed one of my cars into the other? I not sure any one person should even be allowed to own two cars at the same time, let alone complain about the repair bills that go with them. In a flash, my anger vanished and I found myself in fit of uncontrollable laughter. I mean, how lucky one person can get? I owned two cars. Life is good.

After that, I can honestly tell you that I did not spend another second worrying about the repair bill. I simply paid it and moved on. In fact, this story has continued to serve as a reminder to me of how blessed I really am. So the next time I find myself complaining about needing to rake the fallen leaves in my backyard or being concerned that the weather isn't exactly to my liking for my morning run, I hope I remember to be thankful. After all, it's just a matter of perspective.

A Lesson From Chuck Norris On How To Treat People

THE WAY WE TREAT THOSE least important to us reveals our true character. Take Chuck Norris, for example.

Chuck Norris' movie, *Sidekicks*, came out in 1992 and my brother Tim and I had the distinct privilege of hosting him on the last stop of his cross-country, whirlwind, promotional tour.

Our job was to escort him around town from theater to theater and provide crowd control and security. Before the tour began, he had agreed to come by the school to meet some of our students and take a few pictures. Over five hundred people showed up! Because we were pressed for time, we had to push the line through quickly so we could make it to the first theater on time. My wife, Angelina, wanted to meet him, too, so she popped in line along with everyone else. When her turn came, she greeted him, told him her name, mentioned that she was my wife, and said how honored we were to have him visit. Then she moved on down the line.

When it was time to leave the school, we packed into two vehicles–Tim and four of our Black Belts in the lead vehicle, with Mr. Norris, his entourage and me in the limo. I was pretty stoked! I was going to be spending the next five hours riding around in a limo with Chuck Norris! Before we left the parking lot, Mr. Norris looked across at me and asked, "Is your wife Angelina going to be able to join us in the limo? We would love to have her!" My jaw dropped. He just met five hundred people in about half an hour and he remembered her name. Over the next few hours, I looked on as Chuck Norris signed the better part of a thousand autographs during our tour of the local theaters.

I was amazed that he went out of his way to connect with everyone he met and make them feel special. In the limo ride between stops, he could not have been more pleasant. Not even once did I see him show the least bit of irritation with the crowds, the silly questions or the hurried pace. And remember, he had been promoting *Sidekicks* for nearly a month straight with no breaks.

Chuck Norris made an unforgettable impression on me that day. It didn't matter whom he met, how old they were or what they looked like. He treated everyone with sincere respect. He was a class act all the way and a great example of how one should treat others. In my opinion, he deserves all the success life has given him.

And this begs the question, "How do you treat those who are least important to you?" We can all take a lesson from Chuck Norris.

Who is a mighty person?

YEARS BACK, I was in the middle of taping a series of four one-half hour instructional videos for the Martial Arts Industry Association (MAIA). Each video was made up of a combination of Martial Arts drills, skills, teaching tips and a Huddle Discussion for kids. I had just finished the third video and was feeling great about the quality and content.

Experience in front of the camera had shown me that on some days I had it, but on others, not so much. On this particular day, I hit my zone and had only one more video to go. YES!!! I had just finished discussing how a mighty person is one who has control of their emotions and can make friends of their enemies when Sue, my producer, asked to speak with me. We stepped away from the crew and then she quietly told me that, due to technical difficulties, we would have to reshoot the first three videos again. Instantly, a wave of indignation enveloped me. I thought to myself, "How could this happen? Why didn't you fix the problem after the first episode? Didn't you see how good those takes were?" I was livid and just about to let Sue know when it hit me: Who is a *mighty person?*

If I really believed that a mighty person has control of his emotions, then this was a great chance to practice. It also hit me that, not only would I look silly by getting upset after talking about the virtues of self control, if I tried to reshoot the former three videos in a less than empowered state, they wouldn't turn out well. Besides, it was an honest mistake and I have certainly made my share of those. So I took a deep breath, gathered myself, and calmly told Sue, "No problem." We shot four videos in record time and they turned out quite well.

What struck me about this incident was that, somehow, I was able override my initial inclination to become angry. I'm not sure exactly how I did this but, if I successfully overrode my anger once, I can do it again. And so can you.

Yes, a truly mighty person is someone who can consistently control his or her emotions and respond calmly and kindly. So what do you say? Let's get mighty!

I'm a better person after you leave the room.

I AM FORTUNATE to have a great relationship with my two children. Although they are well behaved and respectful when they should be, there is also a playful side to our relationship and we often banter back and forth. One time, my daughter, son and I were having one of our good-natured verbal sparring sessions. My son jokingly told his sister how lucky she was to have him to guide her in the ways of being a better person. She rolled her eyes, smiled and said, "Bro, I'm a better person *after* you leave the room."

I immediately realized that there were two ways this sentence could be interpreted. It could mean that *being around you has affected me in a profoundly positive way* and *I'm a better person for it.* Or, it could mean that *being around you brings me down so much that I'm better off the moment you leave.*

So the question is, "How would the people in your life interpret this line as it relates to you?" I think we'd all agree that when we leave a room, we want the people we just left to feel that their lives are just a little bit better because we had been with them.

Is your guard up or your hand out?

OVER THE YEARS, I've demonstrated to different groups how your attitude can affect others. It is very easy to do. Here is how it works.

I call a person up to the front of the room and ask to give me their first *reaction* to my *action*. After they agree, I step toward them and put my guard up in an aggressive fashion. Inevitably, they respond by putting their guard up.

Next, I extend my hand out in friendship. They always respond in turn. Finally, I ask them to put their guard up.

When it is up, I extend out my hand in friendship. They always give me a blank stare, followed by a handshake.

The point of this drill is to make everyone aware of how easy it is to REACT to the energy of others by mirroring their energy. When they act defensive towards us (guard up), it is difficult not to act defensive back. Likewise, when someone is friendly towards us (hand out), it is pretty easy to return the favor. The real challenge for us lays in the third example. When you cross paths with someone who has their guard up, can you resist the instinct to respond likewise and put your hand out in a gesture of friendship instead? It isn't easy and takes mindful effort, but the results can be stunning.

So the next time you find yourself in a hostile environment, I challenge you to resist your first instinct, no matter how strong, and really try to extend your hand in friendship. You'll be amazed.

The Value of Routine

THIS OLD SAYING IS AS TRUE TODAY as when it was originally written: *Take care of the days and the years take care of themselves.* This concept is so simple, but it is usually overlooked or dismissed in search of something more advanced or complicated.

In their book, *The Power of Full Engagement*, Jim Loehr and Tony Schwartz talk about the importance of developing POSITIVE DAILY RITUALS. They refer to the fact that long-term success is directly related to the number of positive rituals an individual has developed.

Begin by analyzing your day from start to finish. What has become your routine? When do you wake up? What do you eat for breakfast? What books do you read? Do you exercise?

Once you've done this at the end of each day for a week, go back and decide whether or not what you're doing is working well for you. If it is, keep going. If it isn't, what can you do differently?

For example, let's imagine that your morning ritual is as follows: Wake up late. Rush out the door without breakfast. Grab a donut then exceed the speed limit all the way to the office while listening to mindless entertainment radio. How will this morning ritual affect your life if it is repeated daily over the course of ten years?

Now let's imagine instead that your morning ritual is

to wake up early, enjoy a tall glass of water, have a brisk workout and be back in time to read some positive literature while enjoying a nutritious breakfast. How will this ritual affect your life if it is repeated over the course of the same ten years? Ask yourself:

Physically, how will I look different?
Emotionally, how will I feel different?
Professionally, where will I be?
Spiritually, how centered will I be?

Chances are, you can see how different your life would be by just developing a more positive morning ritual. Now let's magnify this concept by imagining a whole day ruled by positive rituals. What would your entire day look like?I encourage you to take the time to write out your ideal day, from waking to going to bed.

Ah, gratitude!

THERE IS NO DOUBT ABOUT IT, running a Martial Arts business can be hard work. I have to wear lots of hats—psychologist, salesman, motivator, teacher, boss and janitor, to name just a few. Even so, I cannot imagine a more rewarding job. We have a chance to impact people's lives for the better every day. But, sometimes, I find this easy to forget when the going gets tough.

My office is located upstairs at our corporate headquarters. Our main school is on the bottom floor. It is 13,400 sq. ft. and has three giant floors for training; and I am extremely proud of it. As a matter of fact, when my brother, Tim, and I first moved our company into this building, I was so excited about this location that I couldn't sleep for a week. After having been there now for so long, I have to admit that there are times I take it all for granted.

So I've developed a daily ritual that helps me remember what my job is all about and how lucky I am to do what I do. Every morning when I first show up at the school, I try to remember what it felt like the very first time I walked in. I wander from room to room just admiring and appreciating our building and all the great experiences that hundreds of students and I have had in this place.

Next, I open my office door, sit down at my desk and take a few moments to remember how blessed I am to do what I love to do. Sure, there are challenges and it's not always easy, but what is that's worth doing? I have found that starting each morning with this ritual has completely transformed my days.

Ah, gratitude! I don't know about you, but it always brings out my best. How do you start your day? Do you let chance control your mood or do you have a ritual that helps to direct it?

Don't be a one-upper.

SEVERAL TIMES IN MY LIFE, I've caught myself trying to outdo someone when it wasn't really necessary or appropriate. For example, a friend of mine was sharing his excitement over a recent four-day vacation to San Diego. Instead of being happy for him, I found myself telling him about my weeklong cruise to Alaska. It may have sounded innocent enough but, upon reflection, it seems that my ego must have found it necessary on some level to one-up him and brag that my vacation was somehow better than his vacation.

I remember witnessing another classic example of one-upmanship at a funeral. I was having a heartfelt moment with the spouse of the deceased when we were approached by a casual acquaintance who interrupted us to say, "I know exactly how you feel. A good friend's father just passed away a couple months ago and it has been pretty hard on me. Don't worry, it'll get easier."

I'm uncertain as to what this person's intent was, but I do know that instead of just supporting the spouse and letting her grieve, this individual found it necessary to let her know that she wasn't the only one who has been through recent heartache—and comparing a good friend's dad passing to that of a spouse seemed insensitive. It felt as if this person were trying to one-up the spouse. At least, this is what it seemed.

I learned something valuable from this incident, though. I vowed to myself at that moment to NEVER be a one-upper again. Since then, I've caught myself many times wanting to say something like, "That's nothing! You know what happened to me?" But then I remember that incident at the funeral and stop myself.

Swapping stories with friends or sharing an occasional anecdote can be fun. However, we should be mindful of our motives for sharing our story. If sharing brings value to the conversation, then great. But if sharing really is just a subtle way of competing with someone, then keep quiet, appreciate the story being told, and offer support, if needed. But for goodness sake, don't be a one-upper!

The Power of Intention

MY FRIEND, Tony Blauer, is a well-known Martial Artist and self-defense specialist. He is the founder of the Spear System and primarily shares his knowledge with law enforcement agencies and the military. His concepts are cutting-edge and I love his teaching. Recently, I had the opportunity to sit in on one of his classes.

During this class, a participant asked him a question regarding the proper form of a certain strike. Tony responded, "Intention makes the technique work, not form. Having good form is fine, but *intention* is what is most important."

I have had the privilege of taking a lesson with my Laido teacher, Shihan Nishiuchi, every other week over many years. As a lifetime Martial Artist who grew up in post World War II Japan, he is steeped in martial knowledge. But what I enjoy most about training with him are the little gems of wisdom that he imparts during virtually every class. These "Shihan-isms," as we refer to them, always have a real-world application. In a recent lesson, he talked about the importance making sure that your words and your INTENT match up. For example, if you say, "Thank you," to someone, mean it. Don't just voice the words. He went on to say that *"INTENT is always more important than words."*

Recently, I have developed a renewed interest in Chi Kung, which roughly translated means "energy work." Chi Kung is a Chinese art designed to promote maximum health. When I was taking a lesson from my friend, Sifu Mark Goblosky, I asked him a technical question about a certain hand positioning, which he answered. But then he said, "Remember Dave, the three most important things about Chi Kung are posture, breathing and INTENT."

I bet you figured out where I am going with this. The power of INTENT is not a new concept. Every great philosopher in recorded history has referred to INTENT. INTENT is a timeless concept. Coach Blauer, Shihan Nishiuchi, Sifu Goblosky, thanks for the reminders.

I am going to recommit to making sure that my INTENT is congruent with my words and actions. Care to join me?

Everything matters.

PERHAPS YOU HAVE HEARD of the *Butterfly Effect?* The Butterfly Effect refers to the idea that a butterfly's wings might create tiny changes in the atmosphere that may ultimately alter the path of a tornado or delay, accelerate or even prevent the occurrence of a tornado in a certain location. The flapping wing represents a small change in the initial condition of the system, which causes a chain of events that lead to larger-scale alterations of events (similar to the *domino effect)*. Had the butterfly not flapped its wings, the trajectory of the system might have been vastly different. While the butterfly does not cause the tornado in the sense of providing the energy for the tornado, it does cause it in the sense that the flap of its wings is an essential part of the initial conditions. Without that flap, that particular tornado might not have existed.

The Butterfly Effect is often used in fiction when presenting scenarios involving time travel and "what if" scenarios ... where one storyline diverges at the moment of a seemingly minor event, resulting in two significantly different outcomes.

The Butterfly Effect can be seen in very simple systems. For example, a ball placed at the crest of a hill might roll into any of several valleys depending on only slight differences of initial position. If anything changes its initial position, even slightly, then the ball's path will change.

Our actions really do matter … all of them. Every decision we make, big and small, affects our future and the future of those with whom we share our world. That is a pretty big responsibility, isn't it? Yes. But it also makes life simpler. (Bear in mind that I said *simpler*, not *easier.*) Being mindfully aware that everything we do matters helps us to shape our decisions both unconsciously and consciously. All we have to remember to do when we are faced with a challenge is to do what is right. Sure, sometimes it is hard to know what is right. But if we are being honest with ourselves, we usually know what the right thing to do is. We just don't always do it. So the next time you are faced with a difficult decision, don't think about the easiest or quickest solution, or the solution that most benefits you. Instead, think about what is right to do and then try your best to do it. Remember, EVERYTHING MATTERS.

Grandpas, Guilt and Gratitude

MY CHILDREN WERE BLESSED to have all four of their grandparents alive, healthy and living close to them when they were growing up. Each grandparent is amazing in his or her own way. Both grandpas are veterans and saw lots of action.

My father, a veteran of WWII, flew eleven missions in the European Theater as a bombardier and navigator before being shot down. He was a prisoner of war for a year and survived two death marches before General Patton freed him. My father-in-law, a veteran of the Korean War, saw several months of combat as an infantryman, advancing on the North Koreans before he nearly lost his life from shrapnel wounds from a hand grenade. Severely wounded, he was shipped home—along with a Bronze Star and Purple Heart—where he underwent several surgeries that would eventually enable him to live a normal life.

I am very proud of both of these men. They are real American heroes who experienced pain and hardships that I can only imagine. I have a great deal of respect for all of our men and women in arms. And I must admit that I've often felt a real sense of guilt for not answering the call of duty and serving my country as a soldier like they did.

In my better moments, though, I understand that guilt doesn't serve anyone well, so I try to shift to feeling a sense of gratitude for all those who have served and are currently serving in the military. That gratitude drives me to want to serve my country and the world in the only way I know how, by trying to be the best teacher, boss, father, friend and husband that I can be.

So what do you feel guilty about? Any chance you can change that guilt into gratitude and let your gratitude drive you to be the best you can be?

Sometimes you just have to say, "Oh, well."

WE LIVE ON A HILL that makes our driveway slightly sloped. Normally, this is not a problem (that is, unless you leave your manual transmission car in neutral and forget to set the emergency brake). Hey, I get it right nine hundred ninety-nine times out of a thousand. It's just that one time in a thousand that's crucial …

For instance, I'd been home for a few minutes when I heard a knock on the door. My next-door neighbor came over to let me know that my car had rolled down the driveway and was in the middle of the street. The back bumper had smashed into our neighbor's tree and was seriously crunched.

My first reaction was to get upset, but then I thought about my friends on the East Coast and what they recently went through with hurricane Sandy. Very quickly, I realized the insignificance of my little mishap. It could've been much worse and it wasn't worth any negative energy on my part. After all, it is going to cost the same to fix the bumper whether I'm upset or not.

Then I remembered what my father told me years ago when I was upset over some other trivial issue. He said, "Dave, if being upset helps solve the problem, then be really upset. But if it doesn't help, why not just calm down and take care of business?" Good advice, Dad. Thanks. I've got to go now. The body shop called and the car is ready.

The Magical Effect of Commitment

I LOVE THIS QUOTE, "Whatever you do, or dream you can do, begin it. Boldness has genius and power and magic in it." (Johann Wolfgang von Goethe) Recently, I was reminded of its truth. I study many Martial Arts disciplines. While I know I still have much to learn, I love all of them and practice them consistently.

One of the disciplines I study is Laido. Laido, considered the peacetime art of the Samurai, is the art of drawing the sword. I have been training under Shihan Nishiuchi and tested for my first-degree black belt in Laido in 2003.

Technically, I should have tested for my second-degree years ago but, truth be told, I wasn't that committed to it. My classmates and I have postponed our test numerous times because we felt we weren't ready or didn't have the time to prepare.

Finally, Shihan Nishiuchi issued us an ultimatum—take the test or he would quit teaching us. At first, I considered discontinuing my lessons. After all, I was an extremely busy person and the requirements needed to pass this test are pretty extreme. But after a bit of thought and a lot of encouragement from my classmates, I decided to go for it. And then I committed.

Interesting things have happened since I recommitted to my Laido training. All of a sudden, I seem to have the time to practice; my skills have improved; and I am sincerely enjoying practicing again. Did I pass my test? Yes! Commitment is an amazing thing.

That won't work for me!

IN MY TRAVELS, I get the chance to meet and work with school owners and Martial Arts professionals from all over the world. I love working with martial artists. Most of them tend to be optimistic, intelligent and open-minded. However, every now and then I meet someone who makes me pause and say to myself, "Really?" The following is the story of that *guy*.

I was teaching an Instructor College in a large metropolitan area in which there is an extremely diverse group of instructors. Some have large schools. Others have small schools. Some are master teachers. Others are just starting out. There were representatives in attendance from a variety of styles and systems and they were all there to learn and grow … except for this one guy.

You know the one. He sat in class all morning, arms crossed, clearly disinterested in anything I or anyone else had to say. I thought that perhaps I was reading him wrong, so during the first break I approached him and asked him a few questions about his school and his background. He gave me a brief history and then said, "I'm not sure why I came today. I was hoping to learn something, but I already know all this stuff you are talking about." Of course, this threw me off my game a bit. I hadn't experienced such bluntness before. I told him that I'd be happy to refund his tuition, if he'd like to leave. He responded by telling me that he was going to stick around and see how it went from there. Although he was a bit better after our conversation, he never fully engaged in the seminar.

When it came time for Questions and Answers at the seminar's end, *that guy* shot down every bit of it.

"I tried that. That won't work in my town," he'd say. "That will never work where I live; people here are different." To make matters worse, he wanted to dominate the floor and talk about himself.

Someone finally blurted out, "You seem to know everything. How many students do you have?" His answer? You guessed it. Not many. He boasted that he'd been teaching for nearly two decades and had forty-five students. But he assured us that all of his students were extremely good because he taught "old-school." He wasn't a "sell out." Honestly, I nearly lost it at this point. It was all I could do to keep myself from jumping up and kicking him in the side of his old-school head.

I had let my guard down. I let *that guy* get inside my head. It took me awhile to calm down. Then my logic kicked in and I decided to learn from it. I asked myself if I have a bit of that same attitude when I'm faced with a new idea or concept that might be hard to embrace. Yes. I might not be quite as obvious or abrasive as that guy, but I can be just as much of a knucklehead sometimes.

So, I decided to do my best be open to others' opinions and viewpoints, and to be receptive to new ideas. I know that I will be better for it. Care to join me?

Choose your battles wisely.

CASPER WAS INCREDIBLY BRIGHT, very fit and extremely witty. He had everything going for him, except for one thing—he always had to be right. He would fight you over the most trivial of details. It was not uncommon at social gatherings to see Casper roaming from group to group looking for a battle. And he was very good at it. He only needed a small opening to state his case, present his findings and then move on to victory.

People who were fully animated in a joyful discussion would suddenly dissipate when Casper approached. Casper was hard to be around. And because of this, he spent a lot of time alone.

The sad thing was that Casper didn't know that winning an argument does not win friends. It was impossible to be around him without putting your guard up and taking a defensive stance.

Whenever I find myself in a possible debate situation, I think of Casper. This is often all I need to do to refrain from engaging in a fight or argument that isn't necessary.

Don't get me wrong. I always try to stand up for what I believe in. But I have learned that when you choose your battles wisely and let trivial differences of opinion go—when you don't pick meaningless fights—people will be more receptive to your ideas when you do speak up.

Thanks, Casper, for being such a great example of what not to do. I will do my best to choose my battles wisely.

Yeah, but I have a hangnail.

MY FATHER USED TO SAY, "Yeah, but I have a hangnail," sarcastically whenever he made excuses for not wanting to do what he should be doing or when he complained about something that was trivial. When I was a child, it embarrassed me. But, as is often the case with parental wisdom, I now find myself telling my kids the same thing. The point is that "I have a hangnail" really puts things into perspective quickly. For example, "Sorry, Honey, I can't take out the garbage now. I have a hangnail." Or if you want to illustrate that you're aware that your complaints are really not as big a deal as you're making them, you could say, "So you think the people in Afghanistan have it rough? Well, I have a hangnail!"

I use this to remind myself that my life is generally good and that my problems pale in comparison with a lot of people's. Don't get me wrong. I have plenty of challenges. We all do. But my challenges are pretty insignificant when you compare them with a neighborhood boy who was paralyzed from a bike accident, or one of the many families who lost everything to Hurricane Sandy, or my friend who went blind shortly after being diagnosed with a rare form of cancer. Those are real problems. Missing a plane, denting your bumper, losing your keys? Really? These are mere inconveniences, nothing more, and we never let mere inconveniences steal our joy.

By the way, did I tell you about my hangnail?

My Formula for Living

RECENTLY, A YOUNG MAN approached me after his Black Belt test to ask me if I had any formula for living based on my life experience. To tell you the truth, he caught me a bit off guard. I wasn't really prepared for his question and gave him some random ideas and half-baked thoughts. Although he appreciated it, I wasn't happy with my response—it got me to thinking that we probably all should have some kind of formula for living, shouldn't we? After putting a good deal of thought into this young man's question, I came up with the formula for living that I would have liked to share with that young man:

1. *Take great care of yourself.* Eat right, exercise, get plenty of rest and find healthy ways to de-stress so you can bring high value to the people in your life. The world needs us at our best.
2. *Treat people right.* Value your relationships. It is always better to have friends than enemies.
3. *Don't be afraid to chase your dreams.* Every worth while accomplishment begins as a tiny seed of thought.
4. *Be prepared to work hard.* Anything worth having is worth working for and rarely do worthwhile things come easily (at least, in my experience).
5. *Don't give up.* There WILL be roadblocks. When you get knocked down, get back up—even when you don't feel like it ... *especially* when you don't feel like it.
6. *Enjoy the process.* Life is too short not to have fun. If this is hard for you to do, nurturing an *attitude* of *gratitude* is a great place to start.

I wish I could tell you that I always follow my own formula for living and never stray, but I can't. I will tell you, though, that I am striving to follow these guidelines to the best of my ability. They have made a **BIG** difference in my life. Why don't you join me?

CHAPTER 3: WHEN THINGS ARE TOUGH

THIS IS MY ALL-TIME FAVORITE QUOTE, *"Be kind, for everyone you meet is fighting a hard battle."* (Philo, circa 20 B.C.) It reminds us that no one is immune to hard times. Every human being ever to walk this earth has experienced adversity. Although some people are born into harder lives than others, no one is exempt or immune from adversity. Challenges are a big part of life. And just when you have met one challenge, another arises, and then another, and then another … As I work through each new challenge, I learn invaluable lessons. It's my honor to share some of the strategies with you that I have found useful along the way. Take heart!

Hang in there. Things will get better.

I'VE BEEN IN THE MARTIAL ARTS business since I was nineteen. While most of my journey has been extremely rewarding and fun, there have been plenty of challenges along the way.

The lowest point in my career was during the winter of 2007-2008. Our plans for a national expansion were proving to be more challenging than we had originally anticipated. The venture capitalist money that we had raised was gone (and there had been a lot of it). We had used it to grow from four locations to twenty in the short span of eighteen months. The next round of financing that we were counting on fell through. The result was a serious cash flow problem. Dave Chamberlain, my business partner, and I couldn't bear the thought of letting down our investors or our staff. We had many sleepless nights as we struggled to figure out how we were going to make payroll and which vendors we would pay each month.

Honestly, Martial Arts training saved my sanity during this time. The daily sessions of grappling, sparring, bag work or kata helped me to escape the gravity of our situation, even if it were just for an hour or two. After working up a sweat, the challenges never seemed as insurmountable —and I was somehow able to look at things from a fresh, centered and optimistic viewpoint.

There was one particular day of training that really helped to transform my thinking and shift my focus. This event helped me not only to believe that there was a light at the end of the tunnel, but it helped me to see it, as well. I was training in Jujitsu. My partner had my back and was doing his best to submit me with the gi choke. The choke was really tight and I experienced a feeling that every Jujitsu practitioner has experienced … that moment when you realize you are in serious trouble. I started to panic and almost tapped out when I was hit with the realization that I could tap if I wanted, but that I didn't have to (at least not yet).

A sense of calm, focused energy overcame me. My mind became clear and I somehow knew that I could get out of this bad situation, if I didn't give up. "Just survive," I thought. And survive I did. Eventually I got out of the choke and reversed my position.

I left the mat that day with a renewed sense of confidence. Sure, we were in trouble. Sure, the future of our company was uncertain. But we didn't have to throw in the towel, at least not yet. And we were not going to give up! We would fight through the challenges with everything we had. With renewed energy, clear heads and focused intent, we proceeded forward. Things eventually got better and, although there continue to be challenges, the future looks bright.

So what's the lesson here? You already know. And so do I. We've heard it a thousand times before. But, sometimes, we just need to remember: *When times are tough and things are challenging, hang in there. Things will get better. You will get through it.*

It is also interesting to note that when you don't give up, life always seems to have interesting ways of rewarding you. In our case, for example, we are now on track with an international expansion. It is just that instead of expanding by increasing our chain of Martial Arts schools, we are expanding by helping existing Martial Arts schools the world over with our Kovar Systems products and ProMAC.

As Winston Churchill said, "Never, ever, ever, ever, ever give up."

NOTE: To all you grapplers out there—don't get the wrong message. It's okay to tap. As a matter fact, it's often good to tap. It means you are out there taking chances, improving your game. But sometimes, well, you know ...

Two Extremes

EVERY MORNING AT THE GYM, I see the same woman doing the same thing—riding a stationary bike ... and I mean **EVERY DAY** since I began going to this gym in 2000! She is always there when I arrive and is still peddling when I leave.

You would think she would be in great shape, but she isn't even close to achieving the fitness level she could attain. I mean no disrespect. It's great that she's there and I'm sure she's getting some benefits from it. But it's evident that she isn't getting the full benefit from working out.

If she's pedaling religiously every morning, how can she be so out of shape? I think it's because she isn't focused on her results. She peddles as slowly as possible and at the lowest level of difficulty and reads while she's exercising. She never even breaks a sweat. When she finishes, her heart rate is probably only a few beats higher than her resting rate. When I asked her how her training was going, she told me that she works out every day, but cannot seem to increase her fitness level because she inherited her father's "slow metabolism."

There is another regular at the gym whose story is quite different. This man is in amazing shape and, if you saw him workout, you would understand why. He is completely focused and trains with incredible intensity. Recently, he broke his leg in a car accident. You would think that would have slowed him down. Instead, he just worked around it. He told me he was going to use his time recuperating to work on some of his weaker areas that he had been meaning to strengthen anyway. It is amazing what attitude, focus and a little hard work can do.

Although these two people share the same gym every morning, they operate in completely different universes. I see these same dynamics and their results in business, too. For example, when I attended the Martial Arts Industry Association convention in Las Vegas, about half of the school owners with whom I spoke told me that they were having a terrible year, while the other half told me they were having one of their best years ever. What was the difference between those who were struggling and those who were thriving?

Most of the business owners who were struggling played the victim. They recounted all the reasons they couldn't be successful. In fact, they were completely convinced that they were helpless and passionately defended the reasons for their non-success, as if they believed the success of their schools was completely out of their control. They were arguing for failure, not success.

The other half of school owners with whom I spoke—
the ones having a great year—admitted to having challenges,
but their attitudes were completely different. They didn't
dwell on their problems, but were mindfully spending time
on the solutions. They understood at a core level that, while
they cannot control the wind, they could adjust their sails.
They inherently knew that they alone held the keys to their
success.

I'd like to say that I'm personally above complaining
and that I'm always focused and working hard, but I am
not. Sometimes, I am tempted to run my business the way
the woman at the gym rides her bike. Fortunately, I have an
amazing team that helps me stay on course. Because we have
seen the great results that come from breaking a sweat and
pedaling hard, I know the hard work is worth it. What about you?

You can always do more than you think you can.

I HADN'T RUN MUCH In a couple of weeks because I was
letting my body heal a bit after my marathon. Finally, I was
ready to get back into my routine of running three miles
around a neighborhood park. I have been doing this run
for years now and it is usually pretty easy for me. But on
that particular day, for whatever reason, I was having a very
difficult time keeping my pace up. And around the two-mile
mark, I was seriously contemplating walking.

Just when I was about slow down, I noticed a runner coming from another trail that connected with the trail I was on. If both our paces stayed the same, we'd collide. I had to choose. Do I slow down and let the other runner get in front of me or do I pick up the pace little bit and get ahead of him?

Although I was pretty tired, I decided to speed up a bit. (What can I say? I guess I'm just a bit competitive). By the time our trails merged, I found myself about ten yards in front of him. He was moving pretty fast but I was determined to keep the lead. I then thought, "What happened to me being tired? Just a moment ago I was contemplating walking and now I'm practically sprinting … and feeling pretty good at that." Then it hit me: *You can always do more than you think you can.* Sometimes we just need a bit more motivation.

Now this epiphany had me thinking about the other areas of my life where I'm tired and am tempted to walk instead of run. I realize now that the trick is to find the metaphorical runner about to collide with me, then pick up my pace and stay out in front.

Well, that's it for now. I have a lot of projects to complete and, for some reason, I've found my second wind.

How is life treating you?

SOME PEOPLE ARE NOT HARDWIRED for personal improvement, while others take to it like squirrels to trees. No matter which category you fall into, you must decide that you want to make your life better and are able to make your life better in order to get to the next level.

I remember Hank, a young man who started training with me in the early eighties. Hank was an incredibly gifted athlete who worked very hard. He had it all going for him—he was handsome, smart and athletic. However, he had one of the worst attitudes that I've ever seen. Hank was always on brink of going over to the dark side and I was constantly trying to pull him back. When challenges arose in his life, he would inevitably take the low road.

As hard as I tried, I was not able to steer Hank off his destructive path. By the age of seventeen, Hank was an alcoholic. By his early twenties, he had added addictions to steroids and Vicodin to his repertoire. At his core, he really was a good guy who was trying his best to do the right thing. But his self-image was warped and he just couldn't keep it together. Amazingly, he still calls me a couple of times of year … usually right after he gets out of rehab. He's now in his forties, but he looks like he's sixty. He has been in and out of jail, never married and cannot hold a job. He has abused his body so much that he is diabetic and has sclerosis of the liver, a condition that will kill him if he continues to drink.

The last time I saw him, I asked, "How's life treating you?" His reply? "Like a baby treats his diapers."

Believe it or not, Hank still believes that *he* doesn't have anything to do with the condition of his own life. To Hank, his condition happened to him and is through no fault of his own.

This makes me wonder … how many times have I pointed the finger elsewhere when challenges arose and did not want to accept the fact that my attitude and actions might have something to do with my situation?

In my better moments, I have this irrational sense of optimism. I know that I hold the key to my own personal improvement. All I have to do is accept where I am and assume full responsibility for it. Then I must decide upon a course of action that will best get me where I want to be. And finally, I need to take action in that direction. All the while, I need to constantly remind myself of all the ways that I have been truly blessed. Is all this simple? Yes. Is all this easy? No. Is all this worth the effort? Absolutely!

By the way, how is life treating you?

Who is the boss of you?

Chances are that some time in your life you have heard a child say, "You're not the boss of me!" I'm not debating whether or not this is an appropriate comment, as it depends on the context. "You're not the boss of me!" raises an interesting question, though. Am I the boss of me? Are you the boss of you?

Your first response is probably, "Of course, I'm the boss of Me. Who else would be?" But there's more to it than that. The truth is that most of us let our urges, impulses and emotions run our life a little more than we should. I believe that BEING THE BOSS OF ME means that the very best of who I am is in control, the part of ME that is patient, compassionate and disciplined. This is easier in theory than it is in reality, but with a little work I think we can all improve.

The easiest way to gain better control of our own lives is to mindfully work on self-discipline.

Self-discipline is merely doing what you should do, regardless of whether or not you want to do it.

I once heard a story of a gentleman who realized that he wasn't in control of his life, so he decided to conduct an experiment. He committed to getting up every morning at 4 AM for one year to go out in his backyard to move a pile of rocks from one place to the other. The next day he would get up again and move the rocks back to their original location. The point of this exercise was to try to develop a higher level of self-discipline. His reasoning was that if he could get himself to follow through with this meaningless and difficult exercise, then he could get himself to do just about anything. The experiment was a success. At the end of the year, this man's level of discipline and the level of control that he had over his life had increased tenfold.

So the big question is: Metaphorically speaking, what is your pile of rocks? What personal discipline can you practice that will help the best YOU be in control of YOUR life? Recommit to it. You'll love the results.

Good judgment comes from bad judgment remembered.

MOST OF US FEEL a combination of confidence and nervousness when we begin something new. We know there'll be challenges ahead. If you're fortunate, you have a mentor or two who can help you by sharing some of the lessons they've learned over the years.

If you've been running a business for a while, you've made some mistakes, learned some lessons, and improved your judgment along the way. And you may be in a position now to mentor someone who is just starting out. As you season and improve, consider that good judgment comes from poor judgment remembered.

If you are mindful of what you've learned along the way, your good judgment will grow along with the success of your company. It's often easier to learn by *doing* than by *hearing*—so while it is sensible to talk with others about their experiences, you may find yourself falling into some of the same difficulties others have faced before you really 'get it.' That's okay … as long as you get it in the end!

One way to consciously develop good judgment is to reflect on each day's events and ask yourself these questions, designed to expose challenge areas and enlighten you on how you can improve. What were my challenges today? How could I have handled them differently for better results? What are my reoccurring challenges? Communication? Money matters? What can I do to improve in these areas?

When you acknowledge each roadblock and the valuable lessons it taught, you can apply your new knowledge to future challenges. When you do this, your good judgment expands into other areas and generates success and growth in both your professional and personal arenas.

Remember going forward that, regardless of your level of experience, you are still going to exercise bad judgment, but no worries because … GOOD JUDGMENT COMES FROM BAD JUDGMENT REMEMBERED.

Don't future-worry.

FUTURE-WORRYING … we all do it and some of us more than others. We worry about the future. Some things we worry about are within our control and other things, well, not so much.

Mark Twain wrote, "I have been through some terrible things in my life, some of which actually happened." Twain was so right! How many times have I worried about something completely beyond my control to the point of losing sleep? Too many times to be sure. Hopefully, I've future-worried less as I've matured. It is not that I don't worry anymore. I still do. It is just that now I do a better job of compartmentalizing my worries. I am reminded of what my mom told me when I was expressing my concern over what is now a forgotten issue. She said, "Son, things are almost never as bad as they seem. You will get through it, I promise you." Mom was right.

So what is a strategy that we can use to keep us from letting our worries get the best of us? Here are some things that I find useful:

1. Decide if your concerns are valid. If they are, do you have any control over the outcome? If not, take a deep breath and say out loud, "I am not going to let something outside my control steal my day." Does this always work? Of course not, but acknowledging this negative emotion is the first step to containing it.

2. If what you are worried about is real and you have control over the outcome, decide on a logical course of action. Then act on it.

3. Try to remain as logical and clear-headed as possible. Remember, logic and emotion are like oil and water; they don't mix. Being overly emotional impairs your good judgment. Here is a quote I play in my head when I am in a negative emotional state: *Never make a decision when you are angry or afraid. It is like letting a coward lead your army.*

4. Take some time to think about past challenges that you successfully navigated your way through or around.

5. Say to yourself, "This too shall pass." Affirm that you WILL get through it and you will be better for the experience. You won't always believe this as you say it, but that's okay. Say it anyway. I have never found a downside to being optimistic and proactive. Yes, some people are naturally more optimistic than others, but optimism is a habit and it can be cultivated (with some effort).

Chances are that things go right for you more often than you think.

How often have you uttered (or listened to) the classic, "You're not going to believe what happened to me" diatribe about a dead car battery, a rude customer, bad restaurant service, being stuck in the world's worst traffic jam, or some other tale of woe?

Yes, things happen. It's natural and perhaps even healthy to vent about such events, from time to time. But if we find it necessary to pontificate about and focus on the bad things that come our way, then we should also give a bit of thought and energy to all of the good things that go right for us for every day.

Some of these good things are big. And some are little. For example, have you entered a packed parking lot only to find the one last spot right up front? Have you grabbed the last bunch of ripe bananas in the store? Were you ever about to run out of gas only to find a service station just in the nick of time AND it was on your side of the road? Did you ever drive all of the way to the store only to realize that you forgot your wallet and then on a hunch, you took a random look into the glove box and found a twenty waiting there for you? I thought so. Me, too. Things like this probably happen to you all the time. The trick is to get in the habit of noticing and appreciating these minor miracles. Go on a treasure hunt to discover everything good in your day, big or small. It's fun. And it will change your life.

So … what happened to you today? Anything special?

The Most Powerful Anti-depressants Available

WHAT ARE THE MOST POWERFUL anti-depressants available? Exercise and service. So the next time you are feeling a bit down, take a dose of both. Even better yet, incorporate exercise and service into your daily routine and watch what happens.

Defend yourself daily against depression. True self-defense is not just defending yourself against the bad guy. It includes defending yourself against sickness, injury, bad attitudes (others' and yours), and apathy … all the stuff that can lead to depression.

For instance, I often don't feel like rising early to go work out. But I try to do it anyway. I always feel great afterwards and am glad that I made the effort in spite of myself. Other times, I might be tempted by that piece of cake on the kitchen counter. I want to eat it, but am so glad when I don't succumb and eat a banana and some berries instead. My body is grateful, too, and says, "Thank you."

So what's the moral? When faced with a choice, always try to do what you *should do*, not what you *want* to do. And how great is it when what we *should do* and what we *want to do* coincide!

I have a long way to go yet, but ever so slowly my self-discipline is getting stronger. And the stronger it gets, the more I get done and the more enjoyable it is to do it. How about you?

Feeling Low or Vulnerable?

EVERYONE FEELS LOW OR VULNERABLE at times, I don't care who you are. And we all, from time to time, need reminding of some basic supporting tips. Here are a few things that I've learned that help me break through the fog when I'm feeling low or vulnerable:

1. Acknowledge and accept where you are. Try not to spend much time in the past. In most cases, our past wasn't as easy as we remember it to be and we weren't as good as we thought we were. Remember that all of your past experiences have brought you to this point. There is only now. And the only direction you can go is forward.

2. Believe that you can make things better. It probably won't be easy, but things rarely are. Can things get worse? Logically if things can get worse, then they can also get better. We all need to lower our guard and allow ourselves to doubt and vent a bit, but it's important to bounce back to believing that your best years still lie ahead.

3. Create or recreate a clear vision of where you want to be. Be realistic but aggressive. Visit this vision on a regular basis.

4. Take consistent action. There is something magical about this. Remember, motivation follows action. You don't have to feel like it, just take action anyway.

5. Stay the course. This isn't baseball where you have only three strikes and you are out. Keeping swinging. You WILL hit the ball eventually.

6. Strive to stay healthy and fit. Everything is easier and flows better when you feel well and are at your best.

7. Count your blessings. Chances are, a lot is going right for you—we just forget to notice sometimes.

The older I get, the better I was.

PEOPLE OFTEN TALK ABOUT how great their lives used to be. They'll tell me that business used to be so much better … that they used to be able to run so much faster … or they used to have much more fun.

While I enjoy reminiscing as much as the next person—it is important to remember where we came from—spending too much time longing for past greatness keeps us from realizing our future potential. This is worth repeating again. *Spending too much time longing for past greatness* (happiness, relationships, etc.) *keeps us from realizing our future potential.* It somehow sends a subliminal message that things will never be as good as they used to be.

But it's important that we send a message to our unconscious that the best years are still ahead of us. If we can affirm this on a regular basis, we set ourselves up for opportunities that we might not otherwise see. We begin to be expectant and move forward.

I've had a great life so far but, in my better moments, I know that the best is yet to be. What are you looking forward to?

CHAPTER 4: MAKING A DIFFERENCE

LET ME SHARE A STORY that you may have heard before. If you haven't, it is worth hearing. And if you have, it will be a good reminder.

One day, a father and his young son were walking along the beach, when they noticed that there were thousands of starfish that had been washed up on shore during high tide. The young boy proceeded to pick them up one by one and throw them back out into the ocean. Upon seeing this, the father told him not to bother because there were way too many starfish and his effort couldn't possibly make a difference. The boy looked at his father, picked up another starfish and exclaimed, "It made a difference to that one!"

I think this story perfectly illustrates the importance of each of us chipping in where we can to make a difference in the lives of those around us. We may not be able to solve every problem, but we can do a lot to ease the burdens that others are carrying. Every little bit helps and, if we all do our share, great things can happen.

As Margaret Mead once said, "Never doubt that a small group of thoughtful, committed citizens can change the world. Indeed, it's the only thing that ever has."

Make me feel important.

I FIRST HEARD *"Make Me Feel Important"* back in 1989 from Zig Ziglar at a seminar in Houston. He was describing how we should imagine a sign on every person's chest with whom we come in contact that reads, MAKE ME FEEL IMPORTANT. He went on to say that we should do this because it is the right thing to do and, by the way, by doing so you will win more business than you can handle.

I experienced the power of "Make Me Feel Important" when I stumbled into Mr. Zigler in the lobby on my way to get a drink of water. It was one of those moments when I asked myself, "Should I talk to him or not?" I decided that I would and built up the courage to tell him about the great time that I was having at his seminar. He proceeded to spend the next couple of minutes asking me about my life, what I do, and where I am planning to go. This was cool, but what really got me was that he seemed sincerely interested in what I had to say. He thanked me for making the trip all the way from California and told me that he had confidence in me and that I would "do great things." I felt great!

Over the years, I have tried to take this concept to heart and do my best to apply it to my business and personal lives. Overall, I thought I'd done okay with this until a few weeks back when I received a clear reminder of how much better I could be at making people feel important.

It was noon and I had just finished teaching a staff class. I spotted one of my former students out of the corner of my eye. I remembered him instantly, even though it had been years since I had seen him. He and his brother used to train with me when they were kids. The brothers were cool and extremely likeable. They both worked really hard in class. The staff and I used to joke about how fearless they were. Both of these boys would spar with anyone. We called them the "heavy hands brothers" because they hit extremely hard for their size.

Back to the story ... I raced out to the lobby to greet him and we had a wonderful reunion. We talked about old times, his family and the amazing success of his brother. You see, after training as a child with me, his brother went on to become a Mixed Martial Arts (MMA) world champion and one of the most recognized fighters in the sport.

After a nice chat, we said our goodbyes and he was on his way. I know he enjoyed our visit and went away feeling appreciated and, maybe, even *important*, because I went out of my way to make him feel so.

Then it hit me. Although I'd like to think I greet all former students the same way, the truth is I don't. Sure, I'm polite. I engage them in conversation, but sometimes I'm not over the top it's-so-great-to-see-you friendly. While I'm hesitant to admit it, the fact of the matter is that I was extra friendly and respectful to this fellow because his brother is famous. It didn't hit me until later on that day and, when it did, I was a bit embarrassed with myself. It was a great reminder to me that we should make the people who cross our paths each day feel important. And then I recommitted to treating the people in my life every day as I treated that young man in the lobby—to make a sincere effort to make them feel important. Anyone care to join me?

Make a conscious effort to believe in one another's success.

I REMEMBER TJ as if it were yesterday. TJ, a young boy from India, was one of my students. He was very bright, but terribly shy. And he was, quite possibly, the most uncoordinated child that I have ever taught. After his introductory lesson, his father asked me point blank, "What do you think? Can he ever be any good at this? Do you think he can ever be a Black Belt?" Not wanting to disappoint the father or lower TJ's self esteem even more, I lied. I told them that, although it would be difficult, I had complete faith in TJ … and I knew that if he stuck it out, he would one day earn his Black Belt. The father responded by saying, "Well, you're the expert. If you believe that he can do it, that's good enough for me. Let's get him signed up."

The guilt started the moment they left and continued to build to the point where I was sick to my stomach. I had completely sold out. There was NO way in this lifetime that

TJ would ever even earn his Yellow Belt, let alone his Black Belt. How could I mislead this nice family? Tim, my brother and business partner, was able to calm me down a bit by reminding me that TJ had no where to go but up and that our program would help even him.

I decided to make TJ my personal project. I made sure to give him lots of attention and encouragement. Every time he was in class, I made it a point to connect with him. I wanted to make sure that he knew that I knew that he was in class. When I began to see how well this approach was working with TJ, I began to make a more conscious effort to connect personally with all my students. Over time, a funny thing began to happen. TJ started to get it! Before long, he successfully passed his Yellow Belt test.

Five years later, there he was standing before me with the rest of our newly promoted Junior Black Belts. TJ had passed the Black Belt test … and quite well, I might add. After the test, he and his dad asked to speak privately with me. The father began to express his appreciation for the program and how much it had done for TJ. Then TJ said, "Thanks for believing in me. I never thought I could do it. I wanted to quit a bunch of times, but I didn't want to let you down. I've learned so much from you. You're a great teacher."

TJ continued to train for a few more years. He grew into a fine young man. The last time we talked, he was in medical school. He wanted to follow in his father's footsteps.

I've lost touch with him now, but I hope our paths will cross again because I never really got the chance to thank him. Looking back, I realize that I learned way more from TJ than he ever learned from me. He taught me how to be a better teacher. He showed me what perseverance really is. He demonstrated the virtues of patience and courage.

So whenever I see someone struggling, I think of TJ and remember to make a conscious effort to believe that he or she will succeed. But I can't stop there. I let them know that I believe in them.

TJ, if you're out there … thank you.

Create positive memories.

AS A MARTIAL ARTS TEACHER, I interact with lots of people every day. And I'm acutely aware that I have a certain amount of influence with my students. I take this responsibility seriously and try to leave my students better off than they were before our interaction. Regardless of where and when I interact with them, I do my best to give each my full attention and leave them with a *nugget*. Hopefully, I'm creating some positive memories for them—or, at least, leaving them with a positive feeling and that sense of acceptance from someone they respect.

I have had a lot of really great role models, people who have created positive memories for me and who have really made an impact on how I live and view my life. Like most people, I've experienced firsthand the negative impact of people who are poor role models, those people who create bad memories for others.

I'll never forget my first day of fifth grade at my new school in January of 1970. We had just moved from Montana to California over the winter break. After being introduced to the class by my new teacher, Mr. O'Brien, I was shown to my desk … my spot for the next several months.

My first interaction with another student was when Barry, the kid who sat to my right, put gum on my seat. At recess he "called me out." I didn't even know what that meant, but I knew it couldn't be good. In fact, for full impact, Barry actually had to explain what "calling me out" meant. Over time, I learned that Barry was fairly harmless; he had a lot of bark but very little bite. I ended up making plenty of new friends and life in California turned out to be okay after all.

Barry's bullying didn't traumatize me for life. But the fact that I'm sharing this story with you means that his poor behavior made an impact on me. I never learned to like him. And we went to school together for years. At one point, Barry tried to be my friend and even invited me over to his house play catch. But I still felt the sting of humiliation as I tried to remove the gum from the seat of my pants in front of the whole class.

If Barry walked into my school today, would I be over-joyed and want to catch up with him? Honestly, no. (Sure, we were kids. It was 5th grade and we all did stupid stuff back then. Most of us probably still do. But I still wouldn't be that happy to see him.) HOWEVER, I would greet him warmly, talk of old times and sincerely wish him well. I would try to create a positive memory for him.

But it wouldn't be the same as seeing Anthony, the kid who stuck up for me on the playground in seventh grade, or Mrs. Austin, my sixth grade teacher who encouraged me when I really needed it. We are all creating memories for others every day. And for those of us who are teachers, even more so.

Years from now, when those you used to know see your picture or hear your name, what memory is going to be jogged?

Let's make some good memories for people every day. Thank you, Barry, for the great life lesson!

The Power of Belief

I LOVE MY PROFESSION OF TEACHING Martial Arts. Based on my experience, I've seen that my belief that each one of my students can succeed is one of the most important factors in their future accomplishments. Numerous studies that have been conducted on the power of believing in someone have reached the same conclusion. Here's a vivid example of the power of belief.

At the beginning of a school year, Mrs. Seiglets, the third grade teacher at Brown Elementary, was brought into the principal's office for a meeting. The principal told her that a special study had been done and they had found that she was the best teacher in the entire school. The principal then told her that as a result she was going to be rewarded. She would be given the very best students in the third grade! The principal explained to Mrs. Seiglets that even though the students' past scores and behavior don't show it, these students were given special tests and they were, in fact, the most gifted students in the school.

At the end of the school year nine months later, Mrs. Seiglets' class did end up with the best grades in the school. Her students' test scores were off the charts. Everyone in the community was amazed with what she had done with these children. When Mrs. Seiglets was brought in and congratulated by the principal, she responded by saying, "Thank you! But remember, I am the best teacher and they are the best students." The principal then confessed, "Well actually, the truth is that this was just an experiment—we don't know if you really are the best teacher in the school or not. We just pulled your name out of a hat and wanted you to believe you were the best teacher in the whole school for the sake of this study. And one other thing, the students were also selected at random."

Think of all the people who have believed in you and how that inspired you to greatness, to pushing your limits and to reaching for the stars. Let's remember the power we hold to help others succeed by believing in them.

CHAPTER 5: FITNESS

FITNESS IS AN IMPORTANT PART of good health. I am amazed at how many smart people don't see the relationship between how they treat their body and their health. You don't pay a price for good health— rather, you enjoy the benefits. When you treat your body with the respect it deserves, it pays you back in spades.

Ideas of what "being fit" means vary, depending on the individual. Hopefully, this section on fitness will help you to find your way to the next level, regardless of where you currently are.

Sports Training and Growing Older

I WAS AT THE GYM doing my thing when a man came up to me and asked, "How do you do it?"

"How do I do what?" I responded.

He replied, "Stay in such good shape at your ... How old are you anyway?"

I believe that what he was trying to say is that he thought I was in pretty good shape for an old guy. He meant it as a compliment. And that's how I took it. I didn't have a clear answer for him at the moment, but his question got me thinking.

Although I'm not old by most people's standards—ask my dad, he just turned ninety—my body definitely operates a little bit differently than did thirty years ago. But it's not just my age that makes the difference; it is also the time I've put in on the mat.

I have been blessed with good genes and good role models. For the most part, I can still do everything that I could do when I was younger. But, after forty years of consistent, relatively hard training, I have acquired some old injuries that affect my performance a bit. Overall, I have nothing to complain about. I just have to be a little more careful now.

Now back to the guy in the gym ... here is what I would have liked to tell him.

There are several things that I find extremely valuable for me in maintaining the best martial arts, health and fitness level possible:

1. Consistency. I rarely, if ever, miss a day of training. I could get away with it when I was younger, but now a missed workout catches up with me quickly.

2. *Warm up completely before adding intensity.* This didn't seem as necessary when I was young but when I neglect my warm-up now, I pay for it later.

3. *The 80% Rule.* I never work out as long as I used to. While I try to work out hard, I always leave the gym or the mat with at least twenty percent of my resources still intact. I like to finish my training session feeling like I could've done a little bit more. This is a good thing. It keeps me from over-training. (If you are younger or training for a fight, this might not be what you need. But as a maturing professional athlete, I think it works perfectly.) Nearly every injury I have had in the last few years of training has been a result of training past my 80% threshold. Fatigue greatly increases risk.

4. *Put health and fitness before your sport.* Don't get me wrong—I love Martial Arts now as much as I ever have. It's just that I want to be able to continue to practice it when I'm really old. And I know that if I train too hard and don't keep health and fitness in mind, an injury is more likely to happen. By keeping

health and fitness my top priority, my Martial Arts skills will only get better with time.

I remember watching a Martial Arts special on TV that was put together by Wesley Snipes. During the show, he honored a bunch of old-school masters. With the exception of Master Jhoon Rhee and Master Ernie Reyes, every one of them was either using a cane or in a wheelchair. I don't want that to be me in twenty years.

Most importantly, I take a few moments at the close of each workout to be consciously aware of just how good exercising feels. Anchoring that good feeling helps me get back into the gym and on the mat on a regular basis. So remember, train smart and put your health and fitness first. If you do, then you'll be able to participate in your sport at the right levels for a long time to come.

Baby-Stepping

I'M A BIG BILL MURRAY FAN. His movie, *What About Bob*, is my favorite. Murray plays the part of Bob, an extreme hypochondriac who is riddled with countless issues. Bob's therapist, played by Richard Dreyfuss, tells him to take *baby-steps*. He explains to Bob that, in order to get better, he needs to build on little victories ... baby-step by baby-step.

I am a strong advocate of health and fitness. I'm at the gym every morning at 5:15 a.m. I don't really like getting up and going to the gym that early, but I love the feeling of leaving at 6:00 AM sweaty and energized. Early morning workouts have become a habit and are an integral part of my very being.

On January 2, I showed up as usual, sleepy-eyed and only half awake. But when I looked up from my workout, I was shocked to see that the gym was packed! As I pondered, I realized that the gym was filled with well-intentioned people who had made New Year's resolutions to exercise more.

Guess what happened next. Within one week, the amount of people working out in the morning dwindled significantly. Within a couple more weeks, the luster and determination for a fit year had worn off and the place was back to the regulars.

What happened? This is my guess. These genuinely well-intentioned people said to themselves, "I need to get into shape. I haven't exercised in years, but starting in January, I'm going to get up early in the morning. I'm going to go to the gym and exercise for an hour 5-days a week. I'm really going to do it this time." But remember, they haven't exercised in years. Once they started going to the gym, they felt tired and sore. Willpower got them through the first week, maybe. Pretty soon, though, even their willpower faded. They began to notice that their other habits that were displaced by the major change—they lost an extra hour of sleep, didn't allow themselves enough time to get the kids off to school, and other challenges. They became overwhelmed by the change and, more often than not, they quit.

So what is the lesson here? Take *baby-steps!* Your chance of success increases dramatically when you set realistic, short-term goals that you can actually accomplish. Instead of taking a major leap and expecting to overhaul your life in one day, start small. Commit to a small change.

For example, if you want to start exercising in the mornings, take baby-steps towards making it a habit. Wake up ten minutes earlier than normal and walk one time around the block. At the end of one week, congratulate yourself. Then step it up a little bit more. Wake up twenty minutes earlier and add a few pushups to your morning regimen. At the end of one week, give yourself a good pat on the back. You get the idea. If you continue to take baby-steps toward your fitness goals, you'll consistently find yourself at the gym every morning at 5:15 am by the year's end. And, voilà, your commitment to fitness has become a habit!

"Take those baby-steps, Bob, baby-steps."

Where are you headed?

JUSTIN QUIT TRAINING with me when he was about twenty years old. He had just finished his second year at a local community college and was off to a university out of state to finish his education. Like so many others before, it was fun watching this small shy boy develop into a confident, 6'2", 200-pound Martial Arts athlete. He was a great student and I was going to miss him, but he promised to stay in touch and keep training while he was away. I was glad to hear that as he had great potential.

I didn't see him again until ten years later. What stood out the most was not the fact it had been ten years, but the fifty pounds that he had put on. At 6'2", he carried it well and was far from obese. I was concerned not about his current weight, but about the direction he was heading. If he kept this up, in another ten years he would be 300-hundred pounds and climbing. Fortunately, he shared the same concern, which is why he had come to see me. He said, "I took a look at the direction I was headed and I didn't like what I saw!"

I'm proud of Justin and happy to have him training with us again. He is a fine young man, recommitted to his health. I am confident that he will succeed. I have been thinking about what he said. We should all probably take a good look at the direction we are heading to see if we like where we're going. Which direction are you headed in?

When it comes to fitness, every little bit helps.

AS A MARTIAL ARTS INSTRUCTOR and fitness consultant, I often hear people tell me that they would like to exercise, but that they just don't have the time or the money for a gym membership. This statement always fascinates me. I don't know if people really believe that they don't exercise because they don't have the time or money, or if it's just an excuse not to exercise.

A lot of people think that, in order to get into shape, they have to join a gym and exercise at least three or four days a week for an hour to get results. They put off all exercise by justifying that *some day* they will have the time or money, but not now. Exercise gets relegated to the bottom on their list of priorities, until their schedules clear.

NEWSFLASH: Although it might be ideal to work out at the gym every day for an hour, you can do a lot on your own in your own environment and in a short period of time.

As of this writing, my father is ninety years old. As one of the last remaining World War II veterans in our area, he is often asked to represent his comrades and his generation at various public events. The remarkable thing is that not only is he still mentally sharp, but he can still fit into his uniform sixty-five years later! Some of this is due to good genes, as both of his parents lived into their nineties. But genes certainly don't account for all of it. My dad has been mindful of his health throughout his entire adult life.

My earliest memory of my father is when I was about three years old—I got out of bed in the morning and, rubbing the sleep out of my eyes, walked into the living room to see my dad doing pushups. He started his habit of daily exercise in the 1950s. His routine is very short—it takes him about eight minutes to get through the whole thing—but he rarely misses a day.

I once asked Dad if he felt that this short workout was even worth doing. After all, you can hardly get warmed up in eight minutes, right? I have never forgotten his response. (It would have been hard to forget it for its sagacity, but also because he repeated it so often throughout my childhood.)

"Son," he said, "a little of something is better than a lot of nothing."

It made sense to me instantly and I apply this concept to many areas of my life to this day. As I was growing up, he taught me to look for ways to sneak in extra exercise. There were little things—like running stairs two at a time whenever you're going to the second floor, or doing a quick set of ten pushups or air squats randomly throughout the day just because or, one of my favorites, balancing on one foot whenever you're stuck waiting in line.

It's amazing how much you can get done when you are mindfully trying to infuse the day with a little more exercise.

(Ideally, this should be in addition to your workout, rather than *replacing* it.) Here are a few more examples: Take the stairs, not the escalator or elevator; walk to the park or the store instead of driving; every other day, do ten pushups and ten air squats every hour; do general household chores with an exercise mindset; or do calisthenics during the commercials when you're watching TV.

Remember, a *little of something is better than a lot of nothing.* I challenge you to come up with your own list. Who knows? With a little luck, maybe we will still fit into the clothes of our youth when we're in our nineties.

The Power of Posture

WHEN I WAS YOUNG, I remember my mom frequently telling me to sit up straight and not to slouch. She may not have been able to explain scientifically why good posture was important, but she understood its value instinctively. Having good posture is important for many different reasons.

First off, having good posture naturally facilitates more effective breathing. It allows the lungs to take in more oxygen and that alone has profound health benefits—it keeps the blood fully oxygenated, which in turn helps your brain and your body function at higher levels.

Good posture also helps your body to work with gravity, rather than against it. Imagine a 20-foot tall flagpole that weighs five hundred pounds. If this flagpole is perfectly straight up and down, it is easy to balance and takes almost no effort at all. However, if you tilt the flagpole just a few degrees in any direction, everything changes. Now you're fighting hard to counteract the effects of gravity.

The same is true of your body. If your posture is bad, your body has to work hard to compensate for it. This puts stress on different parts of the body and can lead to fatigue and injury. But when your posture is straight, you are able to work with gravity not against it.

The key to having good posture is to line up your ears directly over your shoulders, line up your shoulders directly over your hips and, when standing, line up your hips directly over your knees.

Finally, having good posture helps you present yourself in a confident manner. As a Martial Arts instructor, I know that one of the most important things I can teach my students is to carry themselves with confidence. When someone walks, stands or even sits with a confident bearing, they are generally treated with more respect and are much less likely to be confronted by predators.

If your posture is already excellent, congratulations! And keep it up. But if it needs a little work, you can start by spending five minutes a day being mindful of your posture. It may feel a bit odd at first, but over time good posture will feel more natural. After you get used to 5-minutes of good posture each day, extend your time to 30-minutes, and then again to half of each day. Before you know it, you will have formed a healthy new habit and you'll feel and look better for the rest of your life.

CHAPTER 6: Why Now Is the Perfect Time for Martial Arts

Self-Defense

"PRACTICE THE FIGHT so you don't have to" describes the self-defense benefits of Marital Arts. As you train in Martial Arts, you will become more confident in your ability to defend yourself. And as your confidence increases, the need to defend yourself will decrease naturally because you will begin to carry yourself in a more self-assured manner. You will project confidence to everyone around you and will be less vulnerable to predatory behavior. Martial Arts training includes strategic or preventative self-defense, as well as physical self-defense. You will learn how to recognize potentially dangerous situations and avoid confrontations.

Athletic Enhancement

There is a reason why most professional sports teams across all the major sports supplement their training with Martial Arts. Martial Arts training offers several advantages. It is amazingly effective in enhancing general coordination because it uses every part of the body in a balanced way. Upper body, lower body, right side, left side, forward movement, lateral movement and rotational movement are all included in martial arts training.

Fitness

Fitness has three components: strength, flexibility and endurance. Martial Arts training demands a balance between the three. Therefore, people who train in Martial Arts will find their weakest areas greatly improved. Because of the greater balance of strength, flexibility and endurance, there will be fewer injuries while participating in other athletic activities.

Health

While Martial Arts training is great exercise, it's also a lot of fun. Kids don't mind doing it. In fact, they love it! And Martial Arts training includes talking about eating and lifestyle habits, so the kids develop healthy habits that stick with them for life, and grown-ups learn to replace bad habits with good ones.

Concentration

Very few activities engage the mind, body and spirit more than Martial Arts. Because the whole person is engaged, a martial artist's ability to concentrate is greatly enhanced by training. And the improved concentration goes beyond the mat into every other aspect of life.

Respect and Courtesy

Martial Arts techniques are, by nature, designed to injure others when applied. Because of this, Martial Arts instructors greatly stress the importance of respect, courtesy and restraint. It has been proven time and again that people who are skilled in Martial Arts tend to be extremely respectful, considerate and composed.

Confidence

Martial Arts training always increases confidence for two specific reasons. First, there are no bench-sitters. Everyone participates and competes against their own potential, rather than against the other students. Second, Martial Arts training is built on the concept of success—it presents a series of realistic, short-term goals that can be attained quickly, while keeping focused on an exciting long-term goal. Each time a student reaches one of these short-term goals and experiences success, their confidence improves.

Stress Management

Personal stress levels are currently pretty high given what is happening in our world right now. And the stress level of the average person is dramatically higher than in the past. Unmanaged stress can be extremely detrimental to our health, our relationships, and even our job productivity. There aren't many things that can reduce stress better than an intense Martial Arts class. Many Martial Arts students arrive at the dojo stressed from the day's activities. But after class, they leave with a completely different mindset. It feels good to train. And I encourage all our students to anchor in that good feeling they have when they leave. Remembering how good Martial Arts makes them feel makes it easier for them to continue in their healthy routine.

Human Interaction

Human interaction counterbalances technology. In the days of working at home, a million television channels, Facebook and other distractions available online, many people need more live social interaction. Not only do you get that through Martial Arts training, but also find yourself surrounded by positive, high-quality, encouraging people (instructors and co-students alike) who help to bring out your best and keep you focused on the prize.

SATORI OPPORTUNITIES
In the Moment ... At Your Best

IT IS SUCH AN HONOR and a privilege to share with you some of the ideas that have helped me so much along the way. I travel a lot both stateside and internationally. I teach these concepts all over the world. And the concepts in *Brief Moments of Clarity: A Martial Arts Instructor's Guide to Living* have been proven to be universally helpful, regardless of country, age, gender or background. Most of the time, I teach these ideas to martial artists via Martial Arts. But I also give talks, workshops and seminars to organizations and companies ... to any entity that wants their people to be *In the Moment ... At Their Best.* Satori.

To book your Satori Talk, Seminar or Workshop, please call (916) 480-0456

or

email me at:
dave.kovar@kovars.com

You can also get in touch via our website: www.kovarsystems.com

OTHER BOOKS BY DAVE KOVAR

Brief Moments of Clarity: A Martial Arts Instructor's Guide to Living is my sixth book. Here are my others:

A Dad's Toolbox for Better Parenting

The Martial Arts Instructor's Toolbox

15 Powerful Tools for Successful Parenting

School Safe/Street Safe: Common Sense Strategies to Keep Your Family Safe

Healthier Kids/Smarter Kids: Common Sense Strategies to Help Your Child Excel at School

BONUS—TWO 9-WEEK PROGRAMS

I'M SO PLEASED to offer you this special bonus beyond *Brief Moments of Clarity: A Martial Arts Instructor's Guide for Living*. This bonus comprises two chapters. The first is *The Mastery Mindset Daily 3x3s* to help you internalize *The Mastery Mindsets* shared at the beginning of this book and put them into action. Again, we're focused on taking baby-steps, so that you get lasting results.

The second is *The 9-Week Healthy Eating Challenge* to help you begin to eat healthier, baby-step by baby-step. We hope you will be pleasantly surprised at the simplicity of *The Healthy Eating Challenge* and some of the great ideas it includes.

Both *The Mastery Mindset Daily 3x3s* and *The Healthy Eating Challenge* are nine weeks long. We do this on purpose, as we teach them in tandem at our schools. So for double the fun (and the benefit), you can combine Week 1's *Mastery Mindset Daily 3x3* with Week 1's *Healthy Eating Challenge*. Then … continue on in the same manner all the way through Week 9 of both programs. Enjoy!

PUTTING THE MASTERY
MINDSETS TO WORK WITH THE DAILY 3x3s

THE DAILY 3x3s are a powerful process to help you internalize the nine *Mastery Mindsets*. *"3x3"* refers to spending three minutes three times a day internalizing that week's *Mindset*. That's it.

Your Daily *3x3* is based on proven psychological principles that recognize that consistent actions have a strong and lasting impact on beliefs. Remember, as with anything new, it may take a few days before you get comfortable with your *Daily 3x3s*.

There are nine *Mastery Mindsets*, one for each week for nine weeks. To get the most from your *Daily 3x3*, take this week's *Mastery Mindset* and calendar it into your phone or computer three times each day, every day, for one week— once in the morning, then around lunchtime, and the once in the evening. If you do these 3-minute daily exercises three times every day, you'll infuse your life with new energy.

You'll probably find that you integrate some of *The Mastery Mindsets* very easily, while others may be more of a stretch. The most challenging *Mindsets* are the ones that will benefit you the most. Stick with them, even if you're uncomfortable with them.

Each week's *Mastery Mindset Daily 3x3* will include a game plan for that particular week. (You might have fun coming up with additional ways to help yourself internalize each of *The Mastery Mindset*s in your *Daily 3x3s*.)

Trust the *3x3* process. You'll be very glad that you committed completely to the process and applied your full focus when you see the results.

Take Week 1's *Mastery Mindset*, "I can. I will." Schedule "I CAN. I WILL." into the calendar on your phone or computer three times per day for an entire week. Consider your *3x3* time sacred. It's really important to find a place where you can be alone and undistracted for three minutes. Make sure that you eliminate all distractions. Turn off your phone, computer and TV. Find a way to keep track of time (a watch with a second hand is ideal), but don't set an alarm to alert you that your three minutes are up. You don't want to be jolted out of your *3x3*.

Recognize that *3x3* might feel awkward at first, but do it anyway … no matter what. At first, you'll need to trust that the process will work. But before long, you'll realize that you have internalized *The Mastery Mindset*s. You'll feel your mental strength building, week by week, and then you'll be excited to do it each day because you've experienced their benefits.

YOUR MMS DAILY 3x3
GAME PLAN FOR WEEK 1

. . . .

I can. I will.

The Mastery Mindset for Week 1 is "I CAN. I WILL." Your goal for this week is to fully internalize this phrase. This will be your first experience with the *3x3* concept. Here are some guidelines to help you get the most from this week's *Mastery Mindset* – I CAN. I WILL.

1. This weekend, give some thought to what "I CAN. I WILL." means to you. Don't try to do any formal process with it. Just think about it from time to time.

2. Starting Monday with your *Daily 3x3s*, simply hold the phrase in your head, contemplate its meaning and decide how it applies to you at the current time.

3. Think of a challenge that you are currently facing. It can be in the area of health, relationships, work or finances. It might be a big challenge or something seemingly small. Next, apply the concept, "I CAN. I WILL." to this challenge. You are probably not going to come up with a solution on the spot and that's okay. Before you can come up with a solution, you have to believe that you can get through this challenge. The first step is to apply "I CAN. I WILL."

4. If you are having a hard time believing that you can get through this challenge, simply spend a few moments reviewing past challenges that you successfully overcame. Undoubtedly, there have been plenty of past challenges that seemed insurmountable at the time, but somehow you navigated your way through them. The same thing can happen with your current challenge. But first off, you have to believe that you can.

5. Say, "I CAN. I WILL." out loud. Say it different ways. Emphasize different words. Whisper it, too. When you get in your car, close the windows and shout it. (Don't worry about looking silly. If anyone's watching, they'll just think you're on the phone or singing with the radio.)

6. Write, "I CAN. I WILL." at least once during each of your three *3x3* segments every day.

YOUR MMS DAILY 3x3 FOR WEEK 1

. . . .

I can. I will.

You might want to email this week's *Mastery Mindset* and the following *Daily 3x3* to yourself—or write it on a card to keep with you in your purse or wallet, so you have it handy.

1. HOLD the phrase in your head, contemplating how it applies to you right now.
2. THINK of a challenge that you are facing and how this mindset can help you.
3. WRITE it down at least once.
4. SAY it out loud several times, even if you have to whisper it.

YOUR MMS DAILY 3x3
GAME PLAN FOR WEEK 2

. . . .

This challenge will make me stronger.

The Mastery Mindset for Week 2 is "THIS CHALLENGE WILL MAKE ME STRONGER." Your goal for this week is to fully internalize this phrase. Here are some guidelines to help you get the most from this week's *Mastery Mindset—* THIS CHALLENGE WILL MAKE ME STRONGER.

1. This weekend, give some thought to what "THIS CHALLENGE WILL MAKE ME STRONGER" means to you. Don't try to do any formal process with it. Just think about it from time to time.

2. Starting Monday with your *Daily 3x3s*, simply hold the phrase in your head, contemplate its meaning, and decide how it applies to you at the current time.

3. Think of a challenge that you are currently facing. While thinking about that situation, consider how you can apply the concept "THIS CHALLENGE WILL MAKE ME STRONGER" to your current situation. Focus on ways that you will benefit from this challenge in the long-term, just as you have from past challenges.

4. Acknowledge your current challenges. Don't hide from them. Confront them in your mind and affirm to yourself that "THIS CHALLENGE WILL

MAKE ME STRONGER." Understand that this does not mean that you will suddenly overcome your challenges. But by regularly acknowledging your challenges and repeating that "THIS CHALLENGE WILL MAKE ME STRONGER," the statement will become true.

5. Spend some time thinking about the German philosopher Friedrich Nietzsche's statement, "What does not kill me makes me stronger," and how it is almost always true ... if we persevere.

6. Say aloud, "THIS CHALLENGE WILL MAKE ME STRONGER." Say it different ways. Emphasize different words. Whisper it. When you get in your car, close the windows and shout it.

7. Write, "THIS CHALLENGE WILL MAKE ME STRONGER," at least once during each of your *3x3* segments.

YOUR MMS DAILY 3x3 FOR WEEK 2

....

This challenge will make me stronger.

1. HOLD the phrase in your head, contemplating how it applies to you right now.
2. THINK of a challenge that you are facing and how this mindset can help you.
3. WRITE it down at least once.
4. SAY it out loud several times, even if you have to whisper it.

YOUR MMS DAILY 3x3
GAME PLAN FOR WEEK 3

. . . .

I deflect negative energy.

The Mastery Mindset for Week 3 is "I DEFLECT NEGATIVE ENERGY." Your goal for this week is to fully internalize this phrase. Here are some guidelines to help you get the most from this week's *Mastery Mindset*— I DEFLECT NEGATIVE ENERGY.

This weekend, give some thought to what "I DEFLECT NEGATIVE ENERGY" means to you. Don't try to do any formal process with it. Just think about it from time to time.

1. Starting Monday with your *Daily 3x3s*, simply hold the phrase in your head, contemplate its meaning, and decide how it applies to you at the current time.

2. Make a list of people and things that are sources of negative energy in your life. Be ready to deflect their negativity when you encounter them.

3. Visualize yourself as being shielded from negative energy. This can be any imagery that comes to your mind. When you get the image in your mind, take a deep breath and say to yourself, "I DEFLECT NEGATIVE ENERGY," about four or five times. (Remember, you're doing this in private. No one will see you so, as odd as it may seem, trust me on this one.)

4. Make a conscious effort to turn off negativity, wherever it might come from—TV and other media, Facebook, magazines or people. Swing the pendulum as far to the other side as possible for the whole week. In your first *3x3* of the day, review your day in advance and tell yourself that you will deflect any negative input thrown your way.

5. Make a conscious effort not to let any person or any situation steal your joy. Decide in advance that you aren't going to take anything negative personally.

6. Say aloud, "I DEFLECT NEGATIVE ENERGY." Say it different ways. Emphasize different words. Whisper it. When you get in your car, close the windows and shout it.

7. Write, "I DEFLECT NEGATIVE ENERGY," at least once during each of the day's three *3x3* segments.

YOUR MMS DAILY 3x3 FOR WEEK 3

. . . .

I deflect negative energy.

1. HOLD the phrase in your head, contemplating how it applies to you right now.
2. THINK of a challenge that you are facing and how this mindset can help you.
3. WRITE it down at least once.
4. SAY it out loud several times, even if you have to whisper it.

YOUR MMS DAILY 3x3 GAME PLAN FOR WEEK 4

. . . .

I accept positive energy.

The Mastery Mindset for Week 4 is "I ACCEPT POSITIVE ENERGY." Your goal for this week is to fully internalize this phrase. Here are some guidelines to help you get the most from this week's *Mastery Mindset*—I ACCEPT POSITIVE ENERGY.

This weekend, give some thought to what "I ACCEPT POSITIVE ENERGY" means to you. Don't try to do any formal process with it. Just think about it from time to time.

1. Starting Monday with your *Daily 3x3s*, simply hold the phrase in your head, contemplate its meaning, and decide how it applies to you at the current time.

2. Make a conscious effort to watch only uplifting and positive TV shows and read positive books. Reach out to good friends that have had a positive influence on you that you haven't spoken with for some time and rekindle the relationship.

3. Be aware of when you're experiencing any positive emotion and hold onto it for as long as you can.

4. One by one, think about the people and things that are sources of positive energy in your life. Notice how you feel when you think about them. Allow yourself to really enjoy these good feelings.

5. Make sure to accept any compliment given to you with a sincere, "Thank you." (It's very easy to say "Thank you" without thinking about it.) Let compliments and other positive energy completely in this week. Look the person in the eye. Say, "Thank you," and mean it.

6. Say, "I ACCEPT POSITIVE ENERGY," out loud. Say it in different ways. Play with it. Emphasize different words. Whisper it. When you get in your car, close the windows and shout it.

7. Write, "I ACCEPT POSITIVE ENERGY," at least once during each of your three daily 3x3 segments.

YOUR MMS DAILY 3x3 FOR WEEK 4

. . . .

I accept positive energy.

1. HOLD the phrase in your head, contemplating how it applies to you right now.
2. THINK of a challenge that you are facing and how this mindset can help you.
3. WRITE it down at least once.
4. SAY it out loud several times, even if you have to whisper it.

YOUR MMS DAILY 3x3 GAME PLAN FOR WEEK 5

. . . .

I remain calm, even in challenging situations.

The Mastery Mindset for Week 5 is "I REMAIN CALM, EVEN IN CHALLENGING SITUATIONS." Your goal for this week is to fully internalize this phrase. Here are some guidelines to help you get the most from this week's *Mastery Mindset* – I REMAIN CALM, EVEN IN CHALLENGING SITUATIONS.

1. This weekend, give some thought to what "I RE-MAIN CALM, EVEN IN CHALLENGING SITU-ATIONS" means to you. Don't try to do any formal process with it. Just think about it from time to time.

2. Starting Monday with your *Daily 3x3s,* simply hold the phrase in your head, contemplate its meaning, and decide how it applies to you at the current time.

3. Review your day in advance. Consciously think through how you are going to handle any potential situation that in the past might have made you upset. Anticipating challenging situations is a key to remaining calm when they arrive.

4. The easiest way to put this concept into action is to be especially mindful of your emotions. Just be aware when you're becoming angry, frustrated, etc. If you can be fully aware when you are starting to experience negative emotions, you are well on your way to remaining calm.

5. When you become aware of any negative emotion, say to yourself, "I REMAIN CALM, EVEN IN CHALLENGING SITUATIONS."

6. When you are alone, say, "I remain calm, even in challenging situations," out loud. Say it different ways. Emphasize different words. Whisper it. When you get in your car, close the windows and shout it.

7. Write, "I REMAIN CALM, EVEN IN CHAL-LENGING SITUATIONS," at least once during each of your 3x3 segments.

YOUR MMS DAILY 3x3 FOR WEEK 5

. . . .

I remain calm, even in challenging situations.

1. HOLD the phrase in your head, contemplating how it applies to you right now.
2. THINK of a challenge that you are facing and how this mindset can help you.
3. WRITE it down at least once.
4. SAY it out loud several times, even if you have to whisper it.

YOUR MMS DAILY 3x3 GAME PLAN FOR WEEK 6

. . . .

My word is law.

The Mastery Mindset for Week 6 is "MY WORD IS LAW."
Your goal for this week is to fully internalize this phrase.
Here are some guidelines to help you get the most from this
week's *Mastery Mindset*—MY WORD IS LAW.

1. This weekend, give some thought to what "MY
   WORD IS LAW" means to you. Don't try to do any
   formal process with it. Just think about it from time to
   time.

2. Starting Monday with your *Daily 3x3s*, simply hold
   the phrase in your head, contemplate its meaning,
   and decide how it applies to you at the current time.

3. Be completely honest with yourself and with others.
   This doesn't mean that you say everything that pops
   into your mind. What it means is that you say only
   those things that are honest and true.

4. Decide in advance that you will only commit to doing
   things that you fully intend to do. Make sure to follow
   through with action.

5. Spend some time thinking about commitments you
   made but didn't keep. Plan to be especially mindful
   of the commitments you make this week.

6. Think about the parts of your life in which you have highest integrity. And think about the parts of your life where your integrity is not as strong. Think about why this difference exists. Plan to make your word law in all areas of your life.

7. Say aloud, "My word is law." Say it different ways. Emphasize different words. Whisper it. When you get in your car, close the windows and shout it.

8. Write, "MY WORD IS LAW," at least once during each of your Daily *3x3* sessions.

YOUR MMS DAILY 3x3 FOR WEEK 6

. . . .

My word is law.

1. HOLD the phrase in your head, contemplating how it applies to you right now.
2. THINK of a challenge that you are facing and how this mindset can help you.
3. WRITE it down at least once.
4. SAY it out loud several times, even if you have to whisper it.

YOUR MMS DAILY 3x3 GAME PLAN FOR
WEEK 7

. . . .

I'm running my own race.

The Mastery Mindset for Week 7 is "I'M RUNNING MY OWN RACE." Your goal for this week is to fully internalize this phrase. Here are some guidelines to help you get the most from this week's *Mastery Mindset*—I'M RUNNING MY OWN RACE. This weekend, give some thought to what "I'M RUNNING MY OWN RACE" means to you. Don't try to do any formal process with it. Just think about it from time to time.

1. Starting Monday with your *Daily 3x3s*, simply hold the phrase in your head, contemplate its meaning, and decide how it applies to you at the current time.

2. Take a moment to think of the people to whom you most often compare yourself. Recognize when you do this; and when you catch yourself comparing yourself to others, interrupt the comparison and say to yourself, "I'm running my own race."

3. Think about the absurdity of comparing yourself to a pro basketball player, if you are built like a professional jockey. Remind yourself that comparisons are never completely fair and accurate, so you aren't going to compare yourself to others any more.

4. Commit that you will compare yourself to your own potential and not to others from this time forward.

5. Be extra mindful not to pass judgment on other people or other situations. A key indicator is when you find yourself feeling 'better' than someone in some way. Every time you find yourself passing judgment, remind yourself that this is pointless.

6. Say, "I AM RUNNING MY OWN RACE," out loud. Say it different ways. Emphasize different words. Whisper it. When you get in your car, close the windows and shout it.

7. Write, "I'M RUNNING MY OWN RACE," at least once during each of your Daily *3x3* segments.

YOUR MMS DAILY 3x3 FOR WEEK 7

. . . .

I'm running my own race.

1. HOLD the phrase in your head, contemplating how it applies to you right now.
2. THINK of a challenge that you are facing and how this mindset can help you.
3. WRITE it down at least once.
4. SAY it out loud several times, even if you have to whisper it.

YOUR MMS DAILY 3x3 GAME PLAN FOR WEEK 8

. . . .

I bring value to all of my relationships.

The Mastery Mindset for Week 8 is "I BRING VALUE TO ALL OF MY RELATIONSHIPS." Your goal for this week is to fully internalize this phrase. Here are some guidelines to help you get the most from this week's *Mastery Mindset*—I BRING VALUE TO ALL OF MY RELATIONSHIPS.

1. This weekend, give some thought to what "I BRING VALUE TO ALL OF MY RELATIONSHIPS" means to you. Don't try to do any formal process with it. Just think about it from time to time.

2. Starting Monday with your *Daily 3x3s*, simply hold the phrase in your head, contemplate its meaning, and decide how it applies to you at the current time.

3. Make a list of people who are important to you. Write down the ways you currently bring value to those relationships. Then write down additional ways that you can bring value to those relationships. And start implementing them.

4. Make a conscious effort to bring value to all of your relationships. From the most important person in your life to the anonymous clerk where you shop.

5. Go out of your way to do something nice and unexpected for a family member, a friend and even a total
   stranger. Notice how you feel when you do it. Don't
   focus on their reaction. Notice how it made you feel.

6. Think of some of the people who add a lot of value
   to your relationship with them and who bring great
   value to all their relationships. Notice how you feel
   about them. Think about some of the things they do
   and make a plan to do similar things for people.

7. Say, "I BRING VALUE TO ALL OF MY
   RELATIONSHIPS," out loud. Say it different ways.
   Emphasize different words. Whisper it. When you get
   in your car, close the windows and shout it.

8. Write "I BRING VALUE TO ALL OF MY
   RELATIONSHIPS" at least once during each of
   your Daily *3x3* segments.

YOUR MMS DAILY 3x3 FOR WEEK 8

. . . .

I bring value to all of my relationships.

1. HOLD the phrase in your head, contemplating how it applies to you right now.
2. THINK of a challenge that you are facing and how this mindset can help you.
3. WRITE it down at least once.
4. SAY it out loud several times, even if you have to whisper it.

YOUR MMS DAILY 3x3 GAME PLAN FOR WEEK 9

. . . .

I have so much to be grateful for!

The Mastery Mindset for Week 9 is "I HAVE SO MUCH TO BE THANKFUL FOR." Your goal for this week is to fully internalize this phrase. Here are some guidelines to help you get the most from this week's *Mastery Mindset*—I HAVE SO MUCH TO BE THANKFUL FOR.

1. This weekend, give some thought to what I HAVE SO MUCH TO BE THANKFUL FOR means to you. Don't try to do any formal process with it. Just think about it from time to time.

2. Starting Monday, in your *Daily 3x3s*, simply hold the phrase in your head, contemplate its meaning, and decide how it applies to you at the current time.

3. Make a list of 250 things that you have to be thankful for. Start with the big things that are good in your life and work your way down to the smallest things. List as many as you can. Ask others for help. Yes, be sure to get help from others. Tell them that you're making this list and ask for their ideas.

4. Pick someone who makes your life better because they're in it. Select someone who really makes a positive difference for you. Go tell them how much you appreciate them. Do this in person, if possible.

5. Find someone who you feel comfortable with, and talk with him or her about all the good things in your life. It may feel weird at first, but be sure to do this.

6. Write down five things every day that you are thankful for. Remember, don't just think them—WRITE them down in full sentences. For example, "I'm thankful that I have a roof over my head."

7. Say, "I HAVE SO MUCH TO BE THANKFUL FOR," out loud. Say it different ways. Emphasize different words. Whisper it. When you get in your car, close the windows and shout it.

8. Write, "I HAVE SO MUCH TO BE THANKFUL FOR," at least once during each of your *3x3* segments.

YOUR MMS DAILY 3x3 FOR WEEK 9

. . . .

I have so much to be grateful for!

1. HOLD the phrase in your head, contemplating how it applies to you right now.
2. THINK of a challenge that you are facing and how this mindset can help you.
3. WRITE it down at least once.
4. SAY it out loud several times, even if you have to whisper it.

THE 9-WEEK HEALTHY EATING CHALLENGE

WITH SIMPLICITY comes power. *The Healthy Eating Challenge* isn't another fad diet. It's an extremely simple and empowering new way to look what and how you eat. Each week's challenge focuses on developing one *Healthy Eating Habit*. When you adopt all nine *Healthy Eating Habits* into your lifestyle, it will transform your life—including the way you feel and look. As mentioned earlier, you might consider coordinating each of the nine *Healthy Eating Challenges* with the nine *Mastery Mindsets*.

Stay hydrated.

Eat low on the food chain.

Eat fresh and unprocessed foods whenever possible.

Eat smaller portions.

Eat mindfully.

Eat more often.

Being healthy and fit feels better than that junk food tastes.

When it's junk food time, don't overdo it.

Eliminate or reduce something unhealthy from your diet.

HEALTHY EATING CHALLENGE—WEEK 1

Stay Hydrated.

Stay hydrated and make sure that you drink enough water every day to keep your body working correctly. Chronic dehydration is very common. Did you know that dehydration results in fatigue, hunger and irritability? So the next time you find yourself grumpy, tired or very hungry, it might just be that you are dehydrated.

So how much water should you drink? A good rule of thumb is that you should drink half your weight in ounces every day. For example, if you weigh 100 pounds, you should drink 50 ounces of water each day. That might seem like a lot, but it's very easy to do. The key is to drink small amounts of water throughout the day.

When you're thirsty, water should always be your drink of choice. Of course, there may be times when you drink other beverages—coffee, soda or fruit juice, for example. But if you choose to drink any of these, it should be as a treat and not to quench your thirst. Beverages other than water should be enjoyed in moderation.

CHALLENGE

Calculate how much water you should drink every day by dividing your weight in pounds by two. Then drink that number in ounces every day for the next seven days. For example: if you weigh 100-pounds, you should drink 50-ounces of water every day. That equals five 10-ounce glasses. Start your day with at least 10-ounces of water first thing in the morning. This will really help you start your day right. Carry a water bottle with you and constantly sip from it.

. . . .

Things You Should Know

Here are some facts about soda and other sugary drinks that are good to know.

- One Coca-Cola Soda (12 fl. oz.) contains 155 empty calories. Empty calories come from food that is high in sugar and fat but low in the nutrients that the body needs to stay healthy. You might be surprised to learn that one can of regular soda contains the equivalent of $9\frac{1}{2}$ teaspoons of sugar.
- Drinking one can of soda causes a temporary spike in your blood sugar. It does give you a temporary boost of energy, but when your blood sugar comes down, you end up with far less energy than when you started.
- Excessive sugar intake from drinking soda not only leads to unnecessary weight gain, it can also lead to diabetes.

- There are 3,500 calories in a pound. In order to lose OR gain one pound, an individual must either subtract or add 3,500 calories from their diet. That equates to 22.5 sodas. If you drink one soda per day, you could gain as much as 16 pounds in one year. Or if you currently drink one soda every day and decide to give it up, you could lose 16 pounds in one year.

- It takes about 23 minutes of walking to burn the calories in one can of non-diet soda.

- Diet sodas aren't much better. Although they do not have the calories of regular sodas, the chemically derived artificial sweeteners they contain (especially aspartame) may act as neurotoxins and have been linked to headaches, memory problems, anxiety, depression, skin irritations, joint pain and more.

- Fruit juice is high in sugar too. The best thing to do is to eat the fruit instead of drinking fruit juice. If you do drink fruit juice, keep it to a minimum and when you do, mix it with water.

So remember, water is the best thing for you when you are thirsty. And if you're going to drink anything else, enjoy just a small amount for taste, not for thirst.

HEALTHY EATING CHALLENGE—WEEK 2

· ·

Eat Low On The Food Chain.

Eating low on the food chain basically means eating lots of vegetables and fruit. Vegetables and fruit:

- Help to lower blood pressure.
- Reduce the risk of heart disease, stroke, and some cancers.
- Lower the risk of eye and digestive problems.
- Help maintain healthy levels of blood sugar that can help keep your appetite in check.

This week's challenge is about eating the appropriate amount of fresh vegetables and fruit that your body needs for optimum health. Nutritionists agree that a person should have a minimum of five servings of fruits and vegetables every day to stay healthy. Nine servings are considered optimal for most people. One serving size is approximately ½ cup. Most people have an easier time with fruit than they do vegetables, but it's important to include vegetables because they are extremely high in vitamins and minerals and they are generally low in calories. Although fruits also tend to be high in vitamins and minerals, they are higher in sugar. It's almost impossible to eat too many vegetables, but this is not the case with fruit. For this reason, we recommend a two to one ratio of vegetables to fruit.

CHALLENGE

Eat a minimum of five servings of fresh veggies and fruit every day, with at least three of the servings coming from vegetables. Drinks do not count in this challenge. It has to be the real thing. Fresh or frozen is always better than canned or overcooked.

. . . .

Things You Should Know

Despite what you might see in commercials, fruit juice, V-8, and other drinks made from fruits and vegetables aren't nearly as healthy for you as the real thing. It's much better to eat fresh fruits and vegetables. Here are some reasons why:

- One 8-ounce glass of orange juice has well over 100 calories in it. It takes about two and a half oranges to make up that many calories.
- You don't get the other benefits the actual orange has to offer like roughage and the additional vitamins and minerals contained in the roughage.
- The actual fruit will make you full so you are less likely to overeat.

HEALTHY EATING CHALLENGE—WEEK 3

· ·

Eat Fresh And Unprocessed Food Whenever Possible.

What is processed food? It is food that has been chemically altered with additives, such as flavor enhancers, binders, colors, fillers, preservatives, stabilizers, emulsifiers, etc. Generally speaking, if any of the ingredients in food aren't 'natural,' the food is processed. Extremely processed foods (think Twinkies) aren't really even real food at all. They are edible 'food-like' substances.

Processed food isn't all bad. Processing has made the world's food supply much safer to eat and the storage of food a much healthier and more viable option. Processing kills pathogens and extends the shelf life of food. If there were a food shortage or even a famine, processed food items would remain edible and could keep you alive a lot longer than raw food, which rots within a few days.

How can we minimize the amount of processed food that we consume? Here are a few examples and guidelines to apply whenever possible:

- Have an apple instead of applesauce or apple juice.
- Have Grape Nuts instead of Lucky Charms.
- Have a baked potato or salad instead of french fries.
- Use lemon juice or oil and vinegar sparingly on your salad instead of ranch and other "heavy" salad dressings.
- Retrain yourself to eat real food like oatmeal, 100% whole grain bread, pasta, beans and legumes (and of course fresh fruits and vegetables), etc.
- Start looking at the ingredients listed on the labels of food and try to buy foods with fewer ingredients listed.
- Make an extra effort to minimize foods that have lots of hard-to-pronounce, scientific names in their list of ingredients.
- Avoid foods that contain high fructose corn syrup and partially hydrogenated vegetable oil (trans fat).

CHALLENGE

- Replace all white flour products with whole grain products. Make sure the label doesn't just say "Wheat or Multi Grain". It must say "100% Whole Wheat or Multi Grain"
- Replace white rice with brown rice.
- Replace all over-processed breakfast cereal with a more natural, healthy choice.
- Eat fruit instead of drinking fruit juice. If you want juice, try squeezing your own from fresh fruit.
- Eliminate or minimize the use of high calorie condiments like butter and margarine, mayonnaise, BBQ Sauce, etc.

. . . .

Things you should know

Despite the benefits of some processed food, eating processed foods exclusively will almost certainly lead to disease. There is no doubt that our bodies thrive on natural, fresh foods! Fresh and unprocessed foods contain beneficial enzymes and nutrients that are destroyed through processing. Be aware that just because a pill contains the "nutrients" of a whole shopping list of vegetables, it doesn't mean that our bodies derive the same benefit from that pill that we'd get from eating the vegetables themselves. Nutrients, enzymes, and other components of the foods we eat work synergistically. We really don't know how well they work when they're isolated from each other, or when we ingest synthetic versions.

HEALTHY EATING CHALLENGE—WEEK 4

. . . .

Eat Smaller Portions.

One of the healthiest places in the world is Okinawa. The traditional Okinawan diet consists almost exclusively of fresh, unprocessed foods. But that is not the only reason for their high level of health. The Okinawans have a saying, "Hari Hachi Bu," that means *80-percent full*. The idea is that you never stuff yourself. Instead of eating until you're full, you eat until you are not hungry. This takes practice and discipline but the benefits are significant.

Most of us are in the habit of eating until we feel full, but science has proven time and time again that systematic under-eating prolongs life. The idea is not to deprive yourself, but rather to eat a little less than you might be used to eating. It really isn't that difficult. All you have to do is to make a conscious effort to take smaller portions.

CHALLENGE

Make a conscious effort to eat a bit less at every meal. (Kids, this doesn't apply to fruits and vegetables. Don't skimp on those. It applies to things like macaroni and cheese, French fries, potato chips, ice cream, cookies, crackers and sugary cereal.)

. . . .

Things You Should Know

Try using a smaller plate for all your meals. This makes it seem that there is more food on the plate. Research shows us that by doing this, you will automatically eat less.

- Most entrées at restaurants are oversized. Try sharing one entrée with someone else or only eating half and taking the rest to go.
- Replace large smoothies with small ones. Replace a 12" sandwich with a 6", etc.
- Instead of eating until you are full, eat until you are no longer hungry.

HEALTHY EATING CHALLENGE—WEEK 5

· ·

Eat Mindfully.

This week we are going to discuss the importance of *Mindful Eating. Mindful eating* refers to eating in a calm, slow, deliberate way. How do you eat mindfully? Believe it or not, you have practiced mindful eating plenty of times in the past. For example, have you ever been looking forward to a big slice of chocolate cake only to find out that there was only a small sliver left? You probably didn't devour it in one quick bite. More likely, you ate it in small pieces and tried to enjoy every crumb. That's mindful eating.

The bottom line is that when you eat mindfully, you will find yourself eating less and enjoying it more. Here are some things you can do to practice more mindful eating:

- Make sure that you have no distractions during your meals other than good conversation with friends and family.

- When it's time to eat, turn the TV off, put down your book, and step away from the computer.

- Make a conscious effort to chew every bite more thoroughly. For example instead of chewing a bite ten times, try chewing it thirty-five times. Thoroughly chewing your food increases your body's ability to digest it effectively and it also allows you to feel satiated sooner. When you eat too fast, the feeling of being full doesn't kick in until after you've eaten way too much. When you slow down the meal, you will feel full sooner.

- To maximize your mealtime enjoyment, make your environment as peaceful and attractive as possible. Clear the table of clutter, use tableware that looks and feels good. Make sure your food is presented in an attractive and pleasing way.

CHALLENGE

This week's assignment is to eat at least one meal a day mindfully from start to finish. It can be breakfast, lunch or dinner, whichever one works best for you. But it has to be at least one meal per day. For your other meals, make sure you chew the first three bites in a slow, mindful fashion. If you can continue beyond the first three bites, that's great. Slow down your meals. Enjoy them. You'll be glad you did.

. . . .

Things You Should Know

In today's busy world, many Americans often multitask by eating while they do other activities. How many times have we eaten on the run, while driving, watching TV or working? Although we may consider this making good use of our time, this hurry-up method of food consumption actually works against us. Here are four things that happen when we don't eat mindfully:

- When we eat while focusing on another activity, we tend to overeat.
- When we're not paying attention to what we're eating, we tend to make less healthy food choices.
- When we're not eating mindfully, we tend to eat too fast.
- Finally, we miss out on the sheer enjoyment of our meal.

HEALTHY EATING CHALLENGE—WEEK 6

· ·

Eat More Often.

This week we are going to talk about the benefits of eating several small meals a day versus fewer large meals a day. Oftentimes people who are trying to lose weight will skip meals, thinking that because they are consuming fewer calories they are more likely to lose weight. A couple of things happen when you practice this mindset. First off, when you skip a meal your body goes into starvation mode. This basically means that your metabolism slows down and your body tries to retain every calorie it can, in the form of fat. So actually you will get the exact results you were trying to avoid. Secondly, when you skip meals your feeling of hunger is exaggerated. When this happens, the hunger can often offset your willpower and you end up eating anything and everything put in front of you. At the end of the day you almost always will end up consuming more calories than you would have by eating smaller meals throughout the day.

CHALLENGE

This week, your assignment is to eat 5-6 smaller, healthy meals a day. The additional meals might consist of low-fat yogurt and an apple, maybe some carrot sticks and a handful of nuts, or perhaps a bowl of oatmeal and a banana.

. . . .

Things You Should Know

Eating several small meals a day helps for a couple of important reasons. First off, it sends your body a clear signal to keep the metabolism moving fast because the next meal is just around the corner. Also, because there's never a meal too far off, you never feel quite as hungry. This will help you to exercise better self-control and make better choices.

Remember, when we talk about a "meal," were not referring to a three course banquet. We're referring to breakfast, lunch and dinner, just like you normally have (but with smaller portions)—and then we're adding two or three smaller meals or snacks in between.

. . . .

HEALTHY EATING CHALLENGE—WEEK 7

. . . .

Being Healthy And Fit Feels Better Than That Junk Food Tastes.

In this week's challenge, we are going to take a look at how most of us view junk food. Have you ever been to a gathering or party where some of your favorite junk food was readily available? It's okay to indulge a little bit every now and then (more about this in next week's *Healthy Eating Challenge)*. Most of us do from time to time. But it's important not to feel deprived when you don't have your favorite junk food.

Have you ever eaten too much junk food and ended up feeling sick? Most of us have. Was it worth the immediate gratification of taste? Probably not. Next time you're tempted by candy, soda, cake or chips, think of upset stomachs, heartburn and fatigue, and then say to yourself, *"Being healthy and fit feels better than that tastes."* When you look at your food temptations this way, they tend to lose their power over you. When you apply this technique, you won't feel deprived. You'll feel empowered.

CHALLENGE

This week's challenge is to find some of your favorite, unhealthy junk food choices (candy, soda, cake or chips) and take a close look at them. But instead of gazing at them with desire, imagine all of the extra sugar, fat and calories they have. Imagine how good you are going to feel when you don't give in to the temptation.

. . . .

Things You Should Know

Imagine that you're about to go to a party. Before you leave, you look in the mirror and tell yourself that you want to eat healthier and you're not going to eat any junk food at the party. When you get to the party, you see your favorite chocolate cake and think to yourself, "That looks so good! I really wish I could have some. Everyone else is enjoying it, but me." In almost every case, guess what happens? You end up eating the cake and feeling bummed about it later. This happens because willpower alone isn't enough.

The good news is that there is a more effective way to resist the temptation than willpower. Imagine that you go to the same party where they are serving your favorite chocolate cake. But this time, instead of feeling sorry for yourself and being tempted to eat it, you look at the cake and say to yourself, "Being healthy and fit feels better than that cake tastes." Instead of imagining how good it's going to taste, imagine the extra weight around your waist, or that full, bloated feeling you get after eating too much junk food. When you do this, you will find that the chocolate cake has less power over you than it did before. Then, imagine how great you'll feel the next day knowing that you found the strength to resist the temptation. You'll be less likely to feel deprived and you'll appreciate how good it feels to make a healthy choice. Remember, no one ever regrets the piece of cake that they didn't eat.

HEALTHY EATING CHALLENGE—WEEK 8

. . . .

When It Is Junk Food Time, Don't Overdo It.

Being a healthy eater does not mean that you must never, ever again enjoy tasty treats that may not be good for you. That would be no fun. In fact, it's important for you to enjoy your favorite foods from time to time, even if they aren't healthy. The trick is to not overindulge. If you love chocolate cake, enjoy it on occasion. Just be sure to enjoy it less often and in smaller portions. As we've discussed in previous *Healthy Eating Challenges*, you'll enjoy a smaller portion more because you are more likely to be mindful of every last bite.

Most of us don't have the willpower to do this without putting together a clear plan ahead of time. There are several things you can do to put this plan into action. One approach is to designate one day of the week as Junk Food Day. This would mean you do not eat chocolate cake on any other day. It will be easier to refrain because you know that you get to enjoy a small portion on Junk Food Day completely guilt free. This alone will help keep you on track.

CHALLENGE

This week's challenge is to pick one of two choices. The first choice is not to eat any junk food except on your predetermined Junk Food Day. Your other option is to reduce the amount of junk food you eat every day by at least fifty-percent. Make sure that you cut your daily junk food consumption by at least fifty-percent. Otherwise, there would be no challenge. Remember, the word challenge means that it won't be easy.

. . . .

Things You Should Know

Another strategy is to pick one time every day when you are going to allow yourself to have a *small* portion of that favorite junk food. Then be sure stick to your plan. And don't forget that it needs to be a small amount. This is crucial to your long-term success.

Remember, when you are following a predetermined plan and it is time for you to enjoy a little junk food, don't feel guilty. Instead, enjoy yourself and move on.

Finally, remember you can eat anything you want within reason once in a while, but not everything you want whenever you want it.

HEALTHY EATING CHALLENGE—WEEK 9

Eliminate Or Reduce Something Unhealthy From Your Diet.

This is the last week of the *Healthy Eating Challenge*. Hopefully, for the last eight weeks you stretched yourself a bit and developed some healthier eating habits. And hopefully, these are habits you can keep as you move forward in your life. This last week might be the most difficult challenge of all … or it could be the easiest. It all depends on you. Your challenge is to find something in your diet that is less than healthy and completely eliminate it for the next seven days.

Fortunately, science has taught us that it is much easier to replace a bad habit than it is to totally just eliminate it. For example, if you decide to completely eliminate chocolate cake from your diet next week and you are used to eating a slice at eight o'clock every evening, you might try eating an apple at that time instead of eating nothing at all. Substituting a healthier choice will make the process of eliminating the chocolate cake much easier.

CHALLENGE

Pick one unhealthy food that you eat on a regular basis. It might be bacon, red meat, mayonnaise, sour cream, butter, coffee, or sweets. Completely eliminate it from your diet for the next seven days.

. . . .

Things You Should Know

Remember, you don't have to pick from the junk food list. There are probably lots of things that you eat during breakfast, lunch or dinner that you would be better off without. Remember, it's a *challenge* so try to stretch yourself. It's only for a week, so pick something that may not be easy. At the end of the week, you can re-evaluate. Most likely, you'll find that it was easier than you thought it would be. Consider continuing to reduce or completely eliminate the unhealthy food from your diet even after you have completed this Challenge.

CONGRATULATIONS!
YOU MET ALL NINE HEALTHY EATING CHALLENGES!
HOW DO YOU FEEL?

WHY REVIEWS MATTER

IN ORDER TO HELP as many people as possible, I need to get the good news out *there*. And the way to do this quickly is by *reviews*. A review is honest feedback that informs others. It's a great way of spreading the good news quickly and sharing good ideas.

Please consider reviewing *Brief Moments of Clarity: A Martial Arts Instructor's Guide for Living* on Amazon.com. Your review doesn't need to be an essay … just your honest, heartfelt response to my book. A few sentences will suffice.

Will you help me get the word out?

THE PRECIOUS 1%

IN THIS DAY and age, reviews are essential for authors. But only one percent of all the people who read a book will review it. Why? Some people might feel they're too busy to leave a review. Maybe they think they don't know what to say. Or perhaps they do not know the positive impact on others their reviews could have.

But the truth of the matter is that YOUR VOICE IS IMPORTANT AND THAT YOU CAN INFLUENCE OTHERS FOR GOOD. Reviewing is a fast process and it feels really good to share positive energy. I'm confident that you'll know just what to say. And your participation means the world to my team and me.

Thank you so much!